UTAH

KAYENTA
BLACK-ON-WHITE

PYROLUSITE

BLACK PAINT

RED SHALE

WHITE CLAY
YELLOW OCHRE

LIGNITE

GALLUP

OBSIDIAN

BLACK
ASH
AREA

WILLIAMS

KLAGETO
BLACK-ON-ORANGE

ZUNI

FLAGSTAFF

TURQUOISE
LOS CERRILLOS

ARGILLITE

SCOTT AZURITE
SALT

COPPER
CARBONATE

ST. JOHNS
POLYCHROME

CINNABAR

ITE
AXES

PHOENIX

STEATITE

GLOBE

COPPER
BELLS (?)

RED-ON-BUFF
POTTERY

TUCSON

NEW

MEXICO

NUS
RDIUM
RITELLA
CYMERIS

NOGALES

MEXICO

PARROTS
AXES
SHELLS
GREEN SOAPSTONE

COPPER BELLS

Santa Clara County Free Library

CALIFORNIA - WESTERN AMERICANA

REFERENCE

 5816

D

A

Santa Clara Valley Library System
Mountain View Public Library
Santa Clara County Free Library
California

Alum Rock
Campbell
Cupertino
Gilroy
Los Altos

Milpitas {Calaveras
Community Center
Sunnyhills}
Morgan Hill
Saratoga {Quito
Village}
Stanford-Escondido

Research Center-Cupertino
For Bookmobile Service, request schedule

The excavation of a pithouse. San Francisco Peaks in the background.

BLACK SAND

Prehistory in Northern Arizona

GREENWOOD PRESS, PUBLISHERS
WESTPORT, CONNECTICUT

Library of Congress Cataloging in Publication Data

Colton, Harold Sellers, 1881-
    Black sand; prehistory in northern Arizona.

    Reprint of the 1st ed. published by the University
of Mexico Press, Albuquerque.
    Bibliography: p.
    1.   Indians of North America--Arizona. 2.   Arizona
--Antiquities. I. Title.
[E78.A7C73 1973]   970.4'91   73-13454
ISBN 0-8371-7137-7

© *University of New Mexico Press 1960*

All rights reserved

Originally published in 1960 by the University of
New Mexico Press, Albuquerque

Reprinted with the permission of the University of
New Mexico Press

Reprinted in 1973 by Greenwood Press,
a division of Williamhouse-Regency Inc.

Library of Congress Catalogue Card Number 73-13454

ISBN 0-8371-7137-7

Printed in the United States of America

Contents

INTRODUCTION

THIS BOOK *is a synthesis, the culmination of forty-two years of archaeological work in an area surrounding the San Francisco Peaks, the most prominent landmark in northern Arizona. Over the years I have published the results of my labors in more than thirty short papers and two extended memoirs and have supervised the preparation of many others. The published studies have been largely devoted to analysis such as the classification on and statistical studies on pottery and the compilation of other archaeological data. These data I recently summarized in a publication called "The Sinagua," and there the reader will find the detailed information on which I based the conclusions presented in that book. So the two books should go together: one book of analysis and this work of synthesis. Here, without the dull statistics, I have attempted to weld bits of information into a single whole, so that the reader can see the aim of an archaeologist—working with facts, in this case, to write a thousand years of history.*

The title, "Black Sand," refers to a layer of black volcanic ash that covers or at least is found in dunes over an area of about 800 square miles, northeast of Flagstaff, Arizona. The staff of the Museum of Northern Arizona has studied this region from many points of view over the last thirty years and I personally can add twelve years more before the Museum was founded in 1928.

The Museum of Northern Arizona is a regional museum and with its research center occupies over 100 acres three miles north of Flagstaff. It is supported by the Northern Arizona Society of Science and Art, Inc., a non-profit corporation supported by an endowment and memberships. From its inception, research in archaeology, geology and biology has been pursued with vigor. The present work is one of the results.

From the preceding paragraph you may have gathered that the synthesis is based on my work alone. This is not so. Many other persons have contributed facts used to build the story. The bibliography at the end of the book lists all the authors who have been consulted in its preparation. To all of these I am deeply indebted. To the present and past members of the staff of the Museum of Northern Arizona I owe particular gratitude, for I have leaned heavily on the results of their research. Among these persons I mention particularly Katharine Bartlett, Lyndon Lane Hargrave, John C. Mc.Gregor, and my wife, Mary-Russell F. Colton.

BLACK SAND

PREHISTORY IN NORTHERN ARIZONA

V. HUBERT

Fig. 1. The Kana-a Kachina, who is supposed to have lived on the top of Sunset Crater. The Hopi visualizes the small trees on the rim of the crater as this Kachina dancing.

CHAPTER I

Land of the Black Sand

NORTHERN ARIZONA culminates in the towering San Francisco Peaks, the remains of an ancient volcano which rests upon the shoulders of the Colorado Plateau. The Peaks, rising to an altitude of 12,700 feet, are now easy to ascend, for an abandoned motor road makes a fine trail to within a couple of miles of the highest point, whence a rough climb over bouldery scree brings one to the summit. Because the peaks stand alone, the summit, rising five thousand feet above the base, presents a view unobstructed and breath-taking. We see that from the pine-clad base of the mountains the land stretches away and away into dim purple distance. We look down on mesas and into the Grand Canyon; we recognize rivers dimly traced by groves of cottonwoods; and we see the high plateau melting into a distant horizon. Indeed, in many directions, on a clear day, we can recognize mountains two hundred miles away. A circle with a radius of one hundred miles drawn about the mountain will include an area of thirty thousand square miles, a region about the size of West Virginia. On this stage was enacted one of the most dramatic stories that the spade of the archaeologist has ever uncovered in North America, a story which furnishes the subject matter for this book— the drama of the "black sand."

If, from our perch on the rocky peak, we turn our faces to the east, a few miles away we will see, six thousand feet below us, a perfect black cinder cone with a rosy rim, glowing in what seem to be the rays of a perpetually setting sun. In 1879 this so impressed Major John Wesley Powell, the geologist, that he called it Sunset Peak, but it is now more correctly known as Sunset Crater.

Among the three hundred cinder cones which cluster about the San Francisco Peaks, Sunset Crater has most attracted the attention not only of the white man, but also of the Indian. The Hopi Indians living seventy miles northeast of the crater believe that many of their kachinas, beneficent spirits who play such an important part in their mythology and ceremonials, dwell on the forested slopes of the San Francisco Peaks. Before many a kachina dance, in which the spirits are personified, is held in the plaza of a pueblo, a group of Hopis travels to the Peaks, in the old days on foot, now by pickup truck, to place prayer offerings in secret shrines and gather Douglas fir branches to decorate the dancers and the altars. On the way to the Peaks their old foot trail led by Sunset Crater, and it was their custom to deposit an offering in the ice cave at the base of *Polotsmo*, "the red hill," the Hopi name for Sunset Crater. In the ice cave, a collapsed lava tunnel where ice is found even in the summertime, the early white inhabitants of Flagstaff report finding pottery jars which the Indians had offered to their gods. And, according to Hopi belief, one band, the Kana-a Kachinas, lived on Sunset Crater itself. Hopis will point out to you the line of stunted pine trees on the rim of the crater which resembles a line of marching kachinas in a dance.

Yaponcha, the wind god, the spirit of the whirlwind, dust devil, the djinn of the American desert, is said to live in a crack in the lava flow from the crater, where he was once sealed in with corn meal mush by two little war gods of the Hopi, *Po-okong-hoya* and *Balonga-hoya*. Sunset Crater is an important place to the Hopi and is of growing interest to the white inhabitants of Arizona.

In the eleventh century the most highly civilized people in the West dwelt in the Salt and Gila River valleys of Arizona. Here, large irrigation canals crossed the deserts, and there were mud-colored villages much like the towns in parts of Mesopotamia, India, and Egypt today. As we now know from studies of the villages of the Nile, the Tigris, the Euphrates, and the Indus, a large number of communities dependent on a single large irrigation canal means an ordered life, some sort of administration, and leisure to indulge in the arts, religious expression, and play. Extensive irrigation is impossible without organized cooperation. Therefore, these people of southern Arizona, whom today we call the Hohokam, had attained a state of culture above the level of that of most Indian peoples of early North America.

One hundred fifty miles north of the Salt River Valley, at the base of the San Francisco Peaks, lived a much poorer people, whom we will call the Sinagua. They lived in lodges built of timber and covered with earth. The floors of some of the houses were at ground level; in others, where the ground was well drained, the floors were three to four feet below the surface. Agriculture consisted mostly of dry farming and because of the high altitude the cold nights made corn growing precarious.

CHAPTER II

B URIAL IN THE SAND

A.D. 1050–75. We can picture a hypothetical Sinagua man living by an ancient lava flow at the east base of the San Francisco Peaks in such an earth lodge as I mentioned above.

From the edge of this terrace, he overlooked his fields of corn growing in a pleasant little park surrounded by a forest of tall pines. When the snow was melting on the San Francisco Peaks a few miles to the west, and again after the heavy summer rains, a stream of water entered the park, supplying a small pond. Here, his wife dipped water for household purposes into her brown pottery jars, which she carried on her back, with a stout tumpline around her forehead. Sometimes the pond failed and she was obliged to use a spring nearly two miles away at the foot of the mountains. There were summers when the corn crop was good and a surplus was gathered, but corn was difficult to preserve for more than one season, because the earth lodge was damp and the stored corn would often mold. Beans and squash were also cultivated, and in the fall, pinyon nuts and walnuts added to the diet. The nearby mountains furnished a plentiful supply of game, and altogether, there was a variety of good food.

One day when the Sinaguan was working in his field, he felt the earth shake. This movement of the solid earth was deeply alarming and it proved a subject of anxious speculation with his neighbors for several weeks, until a more severe earthquake again disturbed their peace. From that time on, the uneasy earth trembled more and more frequently and the shocks were more severe. They seemed to center in a neighborhood about two miles north of his lodge. Fearing the wrath of the earth gods, he and his neighbors decided to move away. Abandoning their homes, they moved several miles south, where the quivering of the earth seemed less severe. There, he and his family excavated a new pithouse and ventured back to remove the main timbers and roofing from the old home. After they had lived some weeks in the new house, and were somewhat reassured, they were terrified one night by a new and particularly heavy shock followed by a continuous trembling and writhing of the earth. Thunderous explosions came from the north beyond the ridge of cinder hills that bounded the valley, and fine black ash rained into the fireplace through the smoke hole in the roof, sounding like hail to the family cowering within. When the pale dawn came, the Sinaguan crawled cautiously to the top of the hill and was transfixed with horror, for he saw smoke spouting from the ground along a line running from his old cornfield to the base of Two Face Hill. The lake in the valley had disappeared, and where it had been he saw a low hill with a great mouth out of which fiery stones were being hurled into the air. Some of the rocks were even as large as deer. A black cloud hung above the hill and the roar from the crater was deafening. Since a strong wind blew from the southwest, no fragments were falling on the spot where he stood, but soon the wind shifted so that he could not see the site of his old home because of the black sand pouring from the sky. He fled to his home and huddled hopelessly with his wife and baby about the glowing coals of his fireplace while a rain of coarse sand trickled through the smoke hole and the light of day slowly faded.

The earth continued to quiver like a wounded animal and the world was full of horrible noise. The day turned to darkest night and for hours cinders the size of small beans beat down amid torrents of rain. After many hours, the wind changed, the light grew, and the sun came creeping out. During this breathing spell, the terrified inhabitants crawled forth and fled to the south, abandoning their homes

Fig. 2. Sunset Crater, a volcano which, about A.D. 1065, spread black ash over an area of 800 square miles, forming the Desert of Black Sand.

and household goods. Looking back, they could see a great cloud hanging over their country; it was streaked with lightning and at night it glowed with a reddish glare. As the wind carried the clouds off to the northeast, they could see showers of black sand still pouring on the earth.

After a few months, violent activity ceased, the clouds rolled away, and the watchers on the distant hills were astounded to see that a new mountain had emerged, tucked in among the familiar cinder hills. From the summit of this mountain smoke streamed away to the northeast, and for a year or so this continued, until the people grew used to it and the smoke slowly grew less and less and finally died away.

When the volcano was quiet again, the Sinaguan cautiously revisited the site of his most recently abandoned home, where he retrieved some of the belongings he had left behind in his fright. He found his valley covered with a mantle of black volcanic ash several inches deep, through which tender blades of grass and small plants were already pushing up, and when he kicked his foot into the sand he noticed with surprise that the underlying soil was quite damp. He decided to venture farther into the black desolation and set off toward the Little Colorado Valley. All the familiar hills were covered with the black sand which the high winds gathered up in clouds of dust or carried drifting slowly along the ground. No living vegetation showed above this surface except the original sparse covering of juniper trees, now stark and dead. It lay, a vast, black, lifeless desert. To the west, outlined against the sky, stood the rosy top of the newly formed mountain, a tiny wisp of white steam floating from its summit in the clear air.

Since no further activity was shown by the mountain and the earth lay still, his family and their neighbors returned to the site of their second home, and when his pithouse was rebuilt and the rotted timbers replaced with new, he planted his first crop of corn in the cinder-covered fields. When autumn came, he discovered that the crops planted in the soil covered with the layer of black volcanic sand were better than the crops he had grown before the eruption, and he took courage. Then, some adventurous farmer discovered that corn could be grown even on the black lifeless desert between the volcano and the Little Colorado River, where no one, before the eruption, had been able to grow anything. It was found that corn would grow even better on the cinder fields than on the alluvial slopes of the mountain, the place of the earlier fields. In a few years young pine trees were observed taking root among the damaged junipers on the desert of black sand.

Word of this rich new agricultural land reached the Hohokam in the south and other peoples living to the north and east. Many families were attracted and in a few years the early Sinagua were nearly

Fig. 3a. The Desert of Black Sand. Volcanic ash which fell about A.D. 1065 from the eruption of Sunset Crater.

Fig. 3b. The Desert of Black Sand. Sunset Crater shows in the background.

swamped with the visitors who brought new ideas with them. Within a generation, the newcomers were absorbed by the Sinagua. But now the people of the black sand led a life quite different from what it had been before the eruption.

We know by archaeological investigation that word must have reached some Hohokam villages, because Hohokam people from either the Salt River or Verde Valley moved up through the mountains and settled in the black sand country.

We know that the number of people in a village watered by an irrigation canal was limited by the amount of food that could be raised on the irrigable land. An ever-increasing population, with many young people wishing to start a family, must have had a difficult time. With all the land that could be regularly watered from the canal already allotted to families, some young people would be forced to take up marginal land—land that the water would fail to reach in unfavorable years, or land that was waterlogged. Their crops, therefore, were uncertain and they were frequently exposed to starvation.

Naturally a story of free good land in the north would interest these people and some would migrate to the new country. These people were poor and they carried with them what possessions they could and disposed of the rest. They might be compared to a family from the "dust bowl," heading for California in an old battered Ford. Along with their pitiful belongings they carried a few precious jars of red-on-buff decorated pottery. In their minds they carried the method of house construction with which they were familiar, the ceremonies associated with a ball court, and ways of making certain specialized types of pottery.

Traversing the trail up the Verde Valley and through the rugged mountains, they crossed the great pine forests to their chosen land. They were amazed at the extent of the black sand desert, but they had no time to explore. They had to act quickly, for others were arriving and selecting the best land.

For their homes they chose a mesa top which covered some six square miles. To the west of them lived a few groups of natives in pithouses on the side of a small hill which was dominated by a crude masonry fort.

The people from the south found that they were too few to hold their mesa for themselves, and soon families from the country to the east took up land beside them.

At first the Hohokam built houses similar to those they had been accustomed to build in the Salt River Valley, but in a few years they found that the San Francisco Mountain type of deep pithouse was warmer in the cold winters of this high north country. They also discovered that molds grew less rapidly in this damper climate if corn was stored in Sinagua-style masonry granaries aboveground rather than in pits.

Because their religious and social life at home had been centered around the ball court, they constructed one near their new village. Soon the court was copied by their neighbors, and teams from rival areas competed for prestige.

Fig. 4. A model of the ball court near Winona Station east of Flagstaff. Similar ball courts are found in central and southern Arizona. Note walls, end openings and three markers.

A.D. 1125. Within two generations after the eruption, instead of living in pithouses dug into the ground, the Sinagua family was to be found living in a three-room masonry house added to the old granary. The pithouse was abandoned, the roof removed, and the depression partly filled with refuse from the new home. Numerous other flat-roofed houses could be seen among the young pinyon and juniper trees that were growing on the black sand surface, while everywhere the fields of these farmers spread across the land.

Often, the married daughter, instead of building a new house for herself, now added a couple of rooms to the mother's home; and sometimes other families added rooms to the original house for sociability's sake and for protection.

But with the growth in size of the apartment houses, more and more babies died of summer complaint, because the people, having always lived in independent, well-spaced dwellings had no traditions of sanitary disposal of wastes. Fewer children were growing up to supply workers for the Sinagua tribe.

A.D. 1225. A visitor to the Sinagua a hundred years later in the year 1225 would have found a revolution in the black sand area. He would have seen the country covered with the ruins of abandoned farm houses. He would have noted close to the mountains some fair-sized towns, each housing over a hundred persons, but other large towns, like Wupatki, he would have observed, were being deserted by their inhabitants, who left behind a few people too old to travel.

In the Verde Valley to the south he would have noted many large new Sinagua pueblos and he would have seen Sinagua from the black sand area going down the trail into the valley with their possessions. They were emaciated from lack of food and riddled with disease.

The traveler, had he been inquisitive and sought the cause of the trouble, would have found that the crops had failed over a number of years. This failure was not caused necessarily by a lack of rain, but by the gradual removal of the black sand which the high spring winds carried in dust clouds from the level fields and deposited in great drifts in the canyons and in other places. The fields no longer held the water, which now ran off after every heavy rain or evaporated from the hard-packed surface. Therefore the corn crops over a period of years had become poorer and poorer and the ears of corn smaller and smaller, until the families did not have enough to eat.. This was a slow process, covering a period of fifty years.

A.D. 1276–99.   Toward the end of the thirteenth century the annual rainfall became intermittent. Although the black sand had been blown from most of the fields years before, yet a small number of Indians had managed to cultivate the light alluvial soils close to the mountains and so had survived. But now, with the lack of rainfall, the crops repeatedly failed. Drinking water was hard to get. The few survivors, harassed by wandering bands of homeless people, left for better-watered country, never to return.

The Sinagua people experienced a number of crises in the history we have recorded. The eruption of Sunset Crater drove them from their homes. The invasion of alien people seeking farm land pro-duced by the volcanic ash must have been a disturbing element before the newcomers were finally absorbed. Increasing aridity, probably accompanied by the normal spring winds and heavy but infrequent rains, destroyed the volcanic ash cover that made farming possible, causing hunger and pestilence in the early thirteenth century. This aridity culminated in the great drought which caused the final aban-donment of most of the region except about the springs in the Hopi country and along the running streams of the Verde Valley.

CHAPTER III

ARCHAEOLOGISTS AT WORK

WE KNOW that the outline of this story of black sand is reasonably true because we can combine eyewitness accounts of the eruption of cinder cones in other lands with archaeological studies made in northern Arizona.

A cinder cone in eruption is violent while it lasts, but the event is relatively short lived, measured in weeks or months. In various parts of the world men have witnessed such volcanic eruptions and preserved accounts of them for posterity. Pliny's letter to Tacitus describes the eruption of Vesuvius in A.D. 79. The eruptions of Vulcan Island near the island of New Britain in 1937, and of Paricutin in Mexico in 1943, have been reported in a similar pattern. Therefore, if the environment of the volcano is thoroughly known, it is possible to reconstruct a prehistoric eruption with a fair approximation of truth.

In many areas of the Southwest, our archaeological knowledge is based on the work of independent investigators working for a season or two on programs without much relation to those of other archaeologists in the same region. Although much splendid work has been done by this kind of independent study, the advantage of a more integrated and sustained program, such as that carried on by the Museum of Northern Arizona, is obvious. Here, in the area of the San Francisco Mountains, a small group of qualified students has been working for more than thirty years on one integrated project.

Experts in other fields of science have given freely of their time: mammalogists have identified the bones of animals used for food; ornithologists have identified bird remains; conchologists, shells from ornaments; mineralogists and chemists, the material in copper bells, ornaments and pipes; botanists, the plant materials used for food or in making baskets. The scientific cooperation that has been offered is a hopeful sign for the future.

You probably wonder what an archaeological expedition of the Museum of Northern Arizona looks like. Having seen pictures of the expeditions of the Oriental Institute or of the British Museum, you might picture in your mind hundreds of turbaned Arabs in night shirts carrying dirt in baskets under the direction of a white man in riding trousers and a pith helmet, against a foreground of desert and a background of distant palm trees.

Our expeditions are much more modest, and the background quite different. In the first place, the proportion of white collars, if one can say an archaeologist ever has a white collar, to laborers is very much higher. In the second place, the field work is almost at our back door, so that sometimes the workers can even commute to the site of an excavation. Generally, however, a camp is established at a convenient point, perhaps in a grove of tall pines, among low juniper trees, or sheltered from the wind behind a low red mesa on the desert. Sometimes the party lives in tents, neatly arranged in a row, the white-and-blue flag of the Museum gaily flying from a pole; sometimes the crew is lodged in an abandoned ranch house. At the head of the expedition may be the director of the Museum, who plans the project, and who is assisted by a laboratory staff of two or three Museum people. The field party is led by an archaeologist, usually a Museum staff member, aided by an assistant archaeologist who acts as foreman. A technical assistant catalogs the specimens as they are uncovered, and keeps the notes up to date. A cook can make or break the expedition. Four to ten students from different universities, with some archaeological background, do the actual digging for their living expenses. Usually each student is assigned to a project—a particular part of the site—and works there with whisk broom and trowel. He keeps his own records and prepares a report on the section of the excavation assigned to him. Two or three Indians are sometimes employed to sift the dirt, remove it from the site, wash the broken fragments of pottery, and do other work requiring unskilled labor.

The crew digs all day, and in the evening they gather about a table to write up their notes or hold a bull session around the campfire under the stars to discuss the theoretical aspects of the work. In a period of six weeks to four months of excavation, so much valuable information is gathered that it usually takes a year in the laboratory to interpret it and prepare a new chapter of the prehistory of northern Arizona.

The spade of the archaeologist has unearthed from under the black sand in the region about Flagstaff the remarkable story of the eruption of Sunset Crater, revealing the rise of an important center of population which reached its greatest influence at the same time the Norman kings were on the throne of England. We have seen how the eruption of a volcano was responsible for this increase in population; how a primitive folk who lived in scattered earth lodges changed its way of life and drew together into large communities, moving its families into many-storied apartment houses—dwellings having all the conveniences, or lack thereof, of a modern Indian pueblo; and how this change in its mode of life finally led to its doom. We will see how an astronomer, interested in sun spots, dated the events of the history of these people in years of our era by learning to read the record in the rings of trees. In the San Francisco Mountains, because scientists in many fields have cooperated, we have an archaeological history as detailed and complete as that of any region of the United States.

Archaeology is history, but history studied without reference to a written record. Like written history, archaeology has a geographical base on which it rests—the relation of human beings to their environment, the ways in which people meet the conditions of land, climate and food. Archaeology without reference to space, time, and culture is impossible.

To determine the geographical base, this study of the early inhabitants of the San Francisco Mountains began as an archaeological survey. An archaeological survey is a method of study, and as a means of unraveling the past history of a people, it is just as important as digging. The purpose of such a survey is not only to discover the remains of the habitations of man but also to collect and record all the information about them which can be obtained without the use of shovel and pick; and, further, to plot on a map the position of each group of habitations in relation to topography, vegetation cover, soil, and water.

In the study of a site, broken pottery fragments, called "sherds," fragments of stone implements, and loose bits of timber lying on the surface of the ground are collected, and these are taken to the laboratory to be cataloged and stored for future study.

The archaeological survey of the Flagstaff area began in 1916 and has continued for nearly half a century; more than five thousand sites have been recorded in the area of our study. As the collections of surface material, principally potsherds, grew, it soon became evident that the kinds of pottery found on different sites were not always the same, even though the sites were close together. This led us to believe that such sites belonged to different periods of time. When excavation was later undertaken and when the annual rings of timbers found in ruins were studied, the sites were dated, and this hypothesis was proved to be a fact. In this way a chronology, essential to any history, has been established.

For the investigator, making an archaeological survey is a fascinating pastime. He wanders everywhere, into out-of-the-way places where otherwise no one would ever think of going, uphill and down dale, by foot, by horse, by car, or even by boat. It is intriguing because one never knows what will be found. Sometimes there is disappointment, for in some areas sites are scarce and difficult to locate and the going is hard. In other places, the sites are so numerous that hours can be spent in one spot. Compared to golf it is much more fun, for the explorer not only enjoys fresh air but sees new country and has something permanent to show for his effort, but this is probably a matter of personal taste.

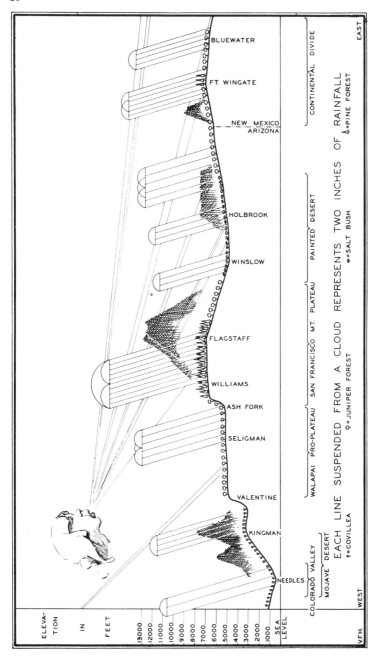

Fig. 5. Mean annual rainfall, physiographic provinces and prevailing wind on a line following the Santa Fe Railroad across northern Arizona.

CHAPTER IV

THE GEOGRAPHICAL BASE AND WORKERS IN THE PAST

THERE IS an old biological axiom, "An animal is part of its environment," which applies not only to the lower animals but to man himself. To understand man's actions we must also understand the region in which he lives.

The state of Arizona contains three major geographical zones—areas whose physical characteristics and landscapes have impressed themselves on the lives of the inhabitants. Most of the northern third of the state is a high, partly forested plateau, 4,000 to 8,000 feet above sea level. Southern Arizona is principally comprised of vast, flat deserts, cut by parallel ranges of cactus-covered mountains—a geographic zone technically described as "basin and range." Between the deserts and the plateau is a region of rugged mountain ridges, cut by deep valleys with flowing streams.

The plateau, mountain, and basin-and-range zones furnish strikingly different environments for man and for the other kinds of animals that inhabit them.

It should be noted that there is yet another zone of importance to our story, although it covers much less territory than any of the three major areas. This is the zone of the ponderosa pine forest, which stretches across the state between the northern plateau and the central mountain region in a band some twenty to fifty miles wide.

A large portion of the plateau of northern Arizona is drained by the Little Colorado River, a muddy intermittent stream receiving its flood waters from desert tributaries, but starting life in the clear brooks of the White Mountains in east-central Arizona. Twice a year, floods pour down its sandy bed—in the spring at the time of the melting snows, and in July and August during the summer rains.

The valley of the Little Colorado cuts northwesterly across the plateau to join the Colorado River in the Grand Canyon. On the right bank of the Little Colorado, rock exposures, mostly of Triassic shales, form a broad band ten to twenty miles wide, almost from source to mouth. These shales and marls, known to geologists as the Chin-le formation, have weathered into many-colored cliffs and domes, giving to the valley the name "the Painted Desert."

In the neighborhood of the San Francisco Peaks, south and west of the Little Colorado, the strata rise in a sloping plain called a monocline. Here the shales have been eroded away, exposing as the surface rock the yellow pebbly Shinarump conglomerate (often hiding uranium deposits), the red Moenkopi sandstones, or where these have been removed by erosion, the hard white Kaibab limestone. During the early Pleistocene age when much of North America was covered by glaciers, the streams from the plateau and the mountains cut in the limestone deep canyons, such as Canyon Diablo, Canyon Padre, Walnut Canyon, and Deadmans Canyon. These streams deposited some of their loads in broad river valleys like that of the Little Colorado, and these gravels are now eroded into terraces.

During the last one million years, volcanic activity has centered around the San Francisco Peaks. Here, beds of volcanic ash and flows of lava covered the limestone surface while basaltic cinder cones dotted the landscape in every direction. Many of the old canyons, such as Walnut and Deadmans canyons, were filled with volcanic debris so that the streams were deflected from their original beds and cut new canyons. It is in this volcanic area that our study of the ancient people of northern Arizona began.

From a low point on the Little Colorado, the country slowly rises in a westerly direction over the forty-mile distance to the San Francisco Peaks. At first one traverses a country of low mesas of red sandstone which stretch to the base of a black escarpment topped by lava flows. After climbing the escarpment of the first flow and crossing some ten miles of flows and fields of volcanic ash, one enters a region of many cinder cones, out of which the San Francisco Peaks (altitude 12,700 feet) rise over five thousand feet above their base to dominate the landscape. The general topographic impression of the valley of the Little Colorado between the river and the San Francisco Peaks is that of a slightly tilted plain, dotted with dozens of volcanoes. An aerial map of the country resembles the surface of the moon.

One of the striking features of the west side of the Little Colorado Valley, in the neighborhood of Flagstaff, is the scarcity of water in regions remote from the river. The underlying rock is Kaibab limestone, covered in some places with thin layers of Moenkopi sandstone, and elsewhere with basaltic lava flows. Except for the Moenkopi formation, which bears a few shaley layers, the rocks are porous, and not one of the many stream beds has a permanent flow of water. Along Walnut Creek, several permanent water holes exist in basaltic canyons. Four seeps issue from the Moenkopi sandstone near the 5,000-foot contour line, and about the base of the San Francisco Peaks there are a few small springs. Several other old springs, now dry, can be located by deposits of potsherds. But, in general, it is a waterless region and quite deserves the name applied to it by the early Spanish explorers, *Sierra sin Agua*, "Mountains without Water."

The "anhydrous" tribe of prehistoric Indians who lived in the black sand country, we have called then "Sinagua." Much of the area covered by the ash-fall now bears a good stand of grass, for the rainfall is ample for pasture. However, because of the lack of water for stock, the area cannot be used fully for grazing, so that much of it is neither inhabited by man nor used by his cattle or sheep. On the other hand, in the eleventh and twelfth centuries, parts of the now waterless area bore a dense human population. As may be inferred from the pottery fragments scattered about them, several springs, which are now dry, seeped water at that time. Therefore, we may conclude that the annual rainfall is now less. Although increasing aridity may account for the failure of certain springs, others may still be seeping under the great banks of basaltic sand.

The climate of the San Francisco Mountains is cool and semiarid, with a succession of dry and rainy seasons. In winter the cyclonic storms which sweep eastward across the continent carry occasional snows. In July and August a monsoon condition brings periodic thunder showers. The spring months, April, May, and June, are dry and windy, and the autumn generally clear and dry, with occasional short rainy spells. These conditions influence agricultural practices. The winter snows melting in the spring supply the moisture to the ground for the germination of seeds and for carrying the sprouting crops through the spring drought, while the summer rains bring the crop to maturity. However, the dry spring winds are hard on growing crops. The blowing sand cuts the delicate stems and the evaporation is excessive. The winds also affected the architecture of prehistoric inhabitants, inducing the people to erect sheltering walls, and the cold winters encouraged them to dig deep pithouses for warmth. We can see how fully the physical environment guided the activities of these people.

As we have seen, it was during the period of human occupation that the eruption of Sunset Crater occurred. The formation, an agglomeration of cinder cones, known to the inhabitants of Flagstaff as the Cinder Hills, caused the establishment of a secondary drainage through Bonito Park and thence northeast to the Little Colorado River. This drainage we call Kana-a Valley. In the unconsolidated yellow oxidized ash that covers the old lava flow on the upper part of the valley, the early inhabitants of the region dug their pithouses. More than twenty-five early sites have been recorded, and many more, now buried by volcanic ash, are suspected.

In a line running from northwest to southeast across this valley, there is a fissure that can be traced for four miles. From this fissure sufficient material was ejected to build the cone of Sunset, 1,000 feet high, to supply two lava flows, to build up a number of fumaroles (small volcanic vents), and to cover about a thousand square miles of the ground surface with black basaltic sand—called ash when the fragments are small. Fragments more than one-fourth inch in diameter are known as *lapilli* (Italian for "little stones") or, more familiarly, as cinders.

The lava flow which issued from the south base of Sunset Crater followed down Kana-a Valley east for some seven miles, and since it is covered with deep ash and cinders, probably occurred a few weeks earlier than the northwestern flow. This eastern flow is known as the Kana-a Flow.

The northwestern, or Bonito Flow, has had a different history. Sunset Crater blocked the drainage of the valley, forming a closed intercone basin into which the basalt poured, creating a lava pond, roughly circular in shape, and about two miles in diameter. About half the lake was formed before the crater ceased to spout ash so that, like the Kana-a Flow, it is covered with black sand and *lapilli*. Near the edges the surface contains fissures that are now filled with basaltic masses to which the term "squeeze ups," or anosma, has been applied. These form the point of origin of secondary flows which are not ash covered. This lava flow is peculiar in another way: the surface is covered with fumaroles, and the basalt has been oxidized red by the action of hot steam over a considerable time. Evidently the activity of Sunset Crater passed through several phases.

Not only was lava poured forth on the surface, but, more important to our story, black basaltic sand, also called ash, was ejected into the air from the crater itself. This ash was carried by the southwest wind and scattered over a wide, roughly elliptical area, with a north-south axis of about thirty-six miles and an east-west axis of about twenty-eight miles. Within this larger oval lies a smaller circular area about twelve miles in diameter, in which the volcanic debris still covers the ground like a black mantle, although on exposed hilltops high winds and heavy rains have carried away even the coarse *lapilli*, and nearly all the black cinder-covered hills show yellow crests. In the outer zone the sand grains are smaller, and the wind has drifted the ash into dunes or blown it into canyons, so that the major part of the open country is clear of volcanic material.

It is this area of black sand that seems to have had such an important effect on the activities of the prehistoric peoples of the plateau.

The determination of the date of the Sunset Crater eruption is a remarkable story of cooperation between the geologist, archaeologist, and tree ring student in attacking a specific problem. The story began in 1931, when the Museum of Northern Arizona was holding a one-man water-color show. The artist was in town at the time and wished to make a painting of Sunset Crater. Since he had no car, Mr. L. F. Brady, our curator of geology, kindly drove him to the region of the volcano and helped him set up his easel on a black cinder-covered hill. Having nothing to do while the artist worked, Brady, in walking about, discovered five pottery fragments on the surface of the cinders. These he recognized as well-known types that belonged to an early stage in Southwestern culture. Of themselves they meant nothing, but taken in connection with an observation made a few days earlier they signified a good deal. The archaeological expedition of the Museum, working at a site just four miles from Sunset Crater, had discovered lens-shaped layers of fresh volcanic ash above the floors of two pre-historic habitations. This could mean but one thing, viz., that the houses were there before the eruption of a volcano. The only volcano recent enough to have supplied this ash was the nearby Sunset Crater. It was possible, therefore, that this volcano might have been active during human occupation of the region. After the discovery of the pottery fragments on the ash field, the archaeological expedition was transferred to this new site. A trench cut through the top of the hill revealed a pithouse directly under an undisturbed level bed of ash. We then knew for certain that man was living in this region before the eruption occurred.

This was only the beginning. A systematic archaeological survey in the cinder-covered area discovered more potsherds. In the ash-fall

Fig. 6. Note the white potsherd among the roots of a tree uprooted by the wind.

area there are no depressions which would call the archaeologist's attention to a pithouse site, because the hollow caused by the collapse of the pithouse walls had been completely filled with wind-blown ash, leaving a nearly level surface. All sherds that were lying on the old surface of the ground are now buried by a foot of ash and *lapilli*. The chance that such a sherd should be transferred to the present surface of this ash is remote and needs explanation. It was fortunate for us that pines flourish in this area and that high winds frequently uproot them. In one case, in the dirt carried up with the roots of a recently fallen pine tree we discovered potsherds that were once buried in the ash. It is now believed that all the sherds found on top of the ash were brought to the surface in this manner. Trees have been falling during all the nine centuries since the eruption of Sunset Crater, but very few sherds reach the surface. Where such sherds are found, a pithouse site is suspected.

Fig. 7. A layer of volcanic ash in a pithouse that was abandoned before the eruption of Sunset Crater in A.D. 1065. The Indian is standing on the floor of the pithouse, pointing to the windblown ash that filled the depression.

Therefore, in order to locate a pithouse, a hole is dug in the ash where potsherds previously have been discovered on the surface. Normally, under a foot of black sand, yellow soil will be encountered. If, however, the shovel fails to reveal yellow soil at two feet, the archaeologist can be pretty sure that he has found a site. Digging down five or six feet to the floor will confirm his suspicions. By these means sixteen sites were discovered and excavated.

But this Pompeii was not a rich city like its prototype in Italy, for the inhabitants were poor Indians with few belongings. And unlike the Pompeians of A.D. 79, they were not caught napping. Indeed, they seem to have had sufficient warning of the eruption, so that they carried their household equipment with them—including even the posts that supported the roofs. We believe that this is so because no household furniture, metates, manos, etc., were found in the houses, the clay floors surrounding the post holes were damaged and very little timber was found. Posts cut with a stone axe represent far greater value in labor than those cut with a steel axe; so it required less labor to remove and carry the posts a few miles than to cut new ones.

By comparing the pottery of those sites buried under the black ash with similar pottery from other sites in which timber had been discovered and dated, the student of tree rings has been able to date the eruption of Sunset Crater as occurring just before A.D. 1070. Thus the geologist, archaeologist, and tree ring student each had a hand in dating the eruption, and an artist, unknowingly, directed the archaeologist to the first buried site.

CHAPTER V

A TIME SCALE
FOR THE ANCIENT SOUTHWEST

THE MOST INTRIGUING and important contribution to the study of archaeology of the Southwest came through the establishment of an absolute chronology, a time scale, expressed in years of our era. One cannot write a history without a time scale of some sort.

Although an archaeological survey can record differences in cultural complexes and can establish roughly a sequence of events, yet it is impossible by this means to determine which end of a sequence is the older. Only by excavation and the study of stratified human deposits can the direction of the sequence be determined and a relative chronology be completed. When trash is cast out of a house upon a dump, the oldest objects are found either at the bottom of the dump or sometimes at the end of the dump nearest the house, because the housekeeper tosses her garbage and ashes at the outer edge of the pile. By studying the objects, particularly pottery fragments from the trash heap, archaeologists had by 1928 built a relative chronology determined by stratigraphy. This was valuable to the historian but gave no dates of our own era.

Through the work of Nelson and others, the direction of the chronological series was determined for the Anasazi cultures of the plateaus of New Mexico and Arizona. Since the terminology applied to the different stages of the series by different authors did not agree, in 1927 a conference of Southwestern archaeologists was held at

Pecos, New Mexico, to define and name these stages. But still, because the ancient peoples of the Southwest had no written languages and so left us no inscriptions to decipher, the establishment of an absolute chronology presented to the early archaeologists an impossible task. The problem was finally solved by an astronomer. And, curiously, it was in the San Francisco Mountains that Dr. A. E. Douglass, then observer at the Lowell Observatory of Flagstaff, initiated the fundamental studies which have led to such happy conclusions.

As an astronomer, Dr. Douglass became interested in the cycles of solar activity which are evident to us in the relative number of sun spots. He found that records of the number of sun spots go back scarcely two hundred years. It has been known for some time that the abundance of sun spots is somehow related to the frequency of cyclonic storms on the earth. Since cyclonic storms usually bring rain and the amount of rainfall is reflected in the annual rings of trees, Dr. Douglass thought that he thus had a method of tracing the sun spot record into the dim past, because some of the big trees in California are more than three thousand years old.

Although these great trees did give a series for more than thirty centuries, yet since they grow in moist places, their climatic record is imperfect. Trees which grow on dry hillsides in semiarid regions are more sensitive to climatic fluctuations. The yellow pines and Douglas firs of northern Arizona and New Mexico give the best records. But these trees are not long lived. The oldest will carry the record back four or five hundred years, but a longer period was required. So Dr. Douglass turned to the timbers in prehistoric ruins then being excavated by archaeologists in regions where yellow pines and Douglas firs were growing. With this material, and by the use of his "bridge method," he built up a chronology of over five hundred years. But he could not attach it to the absolute chronology built from existing trees, and from beams found in the Hopi towns. A beam from the Hopi pueblo of Oraibi carried the chronology back to A.D. 1260. With grants from the National Geographic Society,

Fig. 8. Tree section of Douglas Fir from Site NA 2507 showing tree rings. Narrow rings represent years with subnormal precipitation.

an expedition was organized in 1927 and 1928. Aided by archaeologists, Dr. Douglass collected borings of older timbers from the houses of the Hopi Indians. Archaeologists under his direction also excavated certain prehistoric sites. At the Whipple Ruin in the little Mormon town of Showlow, Arizona, Emil W. Haury and Lyndon Lane Hargrave found a piece of charcoal, the rings of which reached from 1237 to 1380, finally closing the "gap." Thus at one stroke, nearly five hundred years was added to the known Southwestern absolute chronology, carrying it back to about A.D. 700. This allowed the dating of many important ruins in terms of years of our era. Since this time, Dr. Douglass has built up another earlier detached chronology, which was joined to the existing one in 1935, carrying the tree ring chronology nearly to the beginning of the Christian Era.

The chronology of the Anasazi, based on tree rings, is more nearly complete than those of the other cultures that occupied the Southwest. The Anasazi lived in a spectacular country of mesas and canyons and left impressive, well-preserved houses in the shelter of overhanging cliffs. In their buildings, they used pine and Douglas fir trees, which react in a very sensitive way to the vagaries of rainfall and so give the best dates; these logs have been preserved in dry caves for centuries.

Tree ring dating, now formalized into the new and exciting science of dendrochronology, is based on the following principles:

1) In any year most trees in temperate regions have a period of growth in the spring and summer, followed by a period of rest in the autumn and winter. In a cross section of a tree there are alternating rings of light- and of dark-colored wood. Under the microscope, a thin slice from such a section shows that the spring growth is composed of large, light-colored cells, while a ring representing the summer and early fall growth is composed of small dark cells. In most trees the light and dark rings together represent a year's growth.

In semiarid regions, where the seasonal rainfall shows a great deal of variation, the widths of the light rings vary considerably. This variation has been found to correlate with the amount of winter precipitation. After wet winters the light-colored rings of conifers are wide; after dry winters the rings are narrow.

2) In a given region, the width of the rings of individual conifers formed in the same year will be of relatively the same size. If the ring formed in 1938 on one tree on the south slope of a steep hill is narrow, narrow rings for that year will be found on all the trees on that same side of the hill.

3) With certain exceptions, conifers growing in larger areas subject to a similar climate will have ring patterns strikingly alike. Narrow rings and wide rings in different trees will follow one another in the same order. In trees on the San Francisco Mountains the order of narrow and wide rings will correspond fairly well with a similar series of narrow and wide rings in the trees of the Chuska Mountains on the New Mexico–Arizona boundary two hundred miles to the east.

4) Sometimes the order of narrow and wide rings during a given period of time carries such a characteristic pattern that Dr. Douglass has called it a "signature." This signature can be memorized and is an important aid in dating.

We could start, for instance, with a tree cut down in 1938, and record the narrow and wide rings from that date back to the tree's first growth in A.D. 1313. By comparing the sequence of wide and narrow rings of an older tree of unknown date with the sequence from the tree of known cutting date, we can find a place where the sequence of wide and narrow rings matches in both specimens. By recording the rings of a number of trees of the same species, we can average the observed individual variations. Thus we can date the time when the unknown tree was cut. If the life of the unknown tree extended earlier than A.D. 1313, we can then record the sequence of wide and narrow rings previous to 1313. By this "bridge method," Dr. Douglass has carried the chronology back to 11 B.C.

With the chronology now established, archaeologists have dated certain pottery types which show characteristic styles of decoration. These styles therefore become indices of cultural stages, just as certain fossils are selected by geologists as indices of geological stages.

It is interesting to note that when the Southwestern ruins were actually dated by Dr. Douglass, hundreds of years were sliced from the old hypothetical chronology established by guess. It was once believed that the well-known cliff dwellings were constructed two thousand or more years ago; but now it has been established that most of them are not more than a few hundred years old. The dating of certain pottery types by dendrochronology has made it possible to give an approximate date to every prehistoric site in northern Arizona in which pottery is found, whether or not timbers have been discovered there.

The dating of sites by pottery is not limited to northeastern Arizona sites alone, because pottery was an important article of prehistoric trade. Northeastern Arizona pottery is often found on sites in southern and western Arizona and in pueblo sites of New Mexico,

INDEX STYLE	DATE
LINO STYLE	**600 A.D.**
KANA-A STYLE	800 A.D.
DEADMANS STYLE	1000 A.D.
FLAGSTAFF STYLE	1125 A.D.
KAYENTA STYLE	1275 A.D.
JEDDITO STYLE	1400 AD.

Fig. 9. The style of pottery design changed with the centuries. Since pottery is now dated by the tree ring method, these styles are important in dating sites on which no timbers have been preserved.

Colorado, and Utah. For example, Black Mesa Black-on-white, a northeastern Arizona pottery type, is known by tree-ring studies to have been made between A.D. 900 and 1100. When a fragment of this pottery is found in a Hohokam site of the Colonial period in the Salt River Valley, associated with Santa Cruz Red-on-buff, the latter type is thus dated by "association." If a piece is found in central Arizona on a site near Prescott, along with Verde Black-on-gray, another type is dated by association.

The importance of the work of Dr. Douglass to archaeologists cannot be overstressed. He has furnished a tool of the utmost value. Because climatic conditions over the Southwest vary considerably, it has been necessary to construct separate tree-ring chronologies for a number of areas. For example, the tree-ring master chart for the Rio Grande Valley is quite different from the chart for the Flagstaff area.

Dr. Douglass and those who have been his students continue this work in the Department of Geochronology at the University of Arizona.

V. HUBERT.

Fig. 10. A reconstruction of the costume worn by members of the Sinagua tribe. The blanket worn by the man is now at the State Museum in Tucson.

CHAPTER VI

SINAGUA INDIANS
OF THE BLACK SAND COUNTRY

WHEN THE ARCHAEOLOGY of the Southwest is mentioned, the reader usually thinks of cliff dwellings and pueblos. But the builders of those houses were preceded by other folk with more primitive ideas, people who left us few records of their lives except the stone implements which they lost or discarded. Recently, in various parts of America, objects of human manufacture have been found and correlated with some of the last stages of the glacial or pluvial period, 10,000 to 25,000 years ago. Although pre-pottery sites have been located in the black sand area, these early cultures here have not been dated.

From north of Holbrook on U.S. Highway 66, to northwest of Cameron on U.S. Highway 89, the eroded remnants of an early or middle Pleistocene bed of the Little Colorado River can be recognized in certain places on one side or the other of the present river course. This ancient river bed now appears as rounded hills, covered with a desert pavement of quartzite pebbles. When trenched, the old river bed reveals gravels and sand from which elephant bones occasionally have been recovered. On the tops of these rounded, gravel-covered hills, sites have been discovered in which crude stone implements and discarded flakes have been found without associated pottery. Over fifty such sites have been recorded in one area on the archaeological survey.

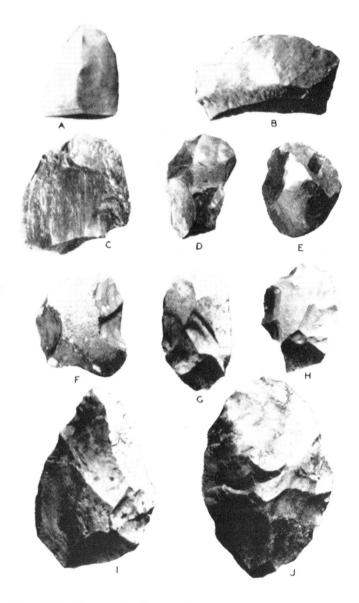

Fig. 11. Primitive stone implements from the Little Colorado Valley. *a* and *d*, scrapers; *b*, side scraper; *c*, chopper; *e* and *f*, end scrapers (plane-like); *g*, *h*, *i*, and *j*, hand axes.

Since many of the implements are very crude the question naturally arises, "Are they man-made or just the phenomena of nature?"

There are several reasons why they are considered the handiwork of man. The implements are found, not on all the gravel hills, but only on certain ones. The distribution does not correspond to the distribution of the gravels, as it would if the implements were "natural." The flakes are not smoothed and worn in such a way as to indicate river transportation. They are found only on the surface, never deeply buried in the gravels. And, finally, many show the cones of percussion that are produced when a pebble has been sharply struck with another stone. Cones of percussion and bulbs of percussion can be made only by a violent blow—a blow that never could have occurred in a stream flowing gently over beds of sand. However, we must not overlook the fact that there is a natural method of producing cones of percussion. The late Professor Laudermilk of Pomona College has shown that lightning striking a cobblestone of quartzite or other hard rock will form such a cone. But the cone created by lightning is formed at random and is not associated with other flaking on the fragment of the cobblestone. Implements usually show secondary flaking and are of common types recognized by archaeologists the world over as the work of man.

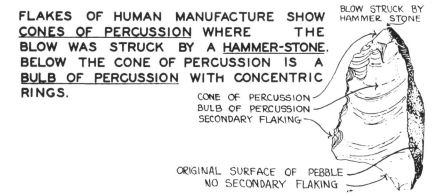

FLAKES OF HUMAN MANUFACTURE SHOW CONES OF PERCUSSION WHERE THE BLOW WAS STRUCK BY A HAMMER-STONE. BELOW THE CONE OF PERCUSSION IS A BULB OF PERCUSSION WITH CONCENTRIC RINGS.

BLOW STRUCK BY HAMMER STONE

CONE OF PERCUSSION
BULB OF PERCUSSION
SECONDARY FLAKING

ORIGINAL SURFACE OF PEBBLE
NO SECONDARY FLAKING

Fig. 12. Flakes of human manufacture show cones of percussion.

The principal features of this culture can be expressed best in negatives. The stone implements show evidences of percussion flaking and no pressure flaking, which means that flakes were produced by sharply striking a homogeneous rock with another rock, rather than by gentle pressure applied with a piece of bone. The implements are found on the surface, never in the gravels, and are not associated with pottery.

The first conference of Southwestern archaeologists, at Pecos in 1927, recognized a series of stages of cultural development which included a hypothetical stage, then unknown, when the inhabitants of the Southwest hunted game and gathered wild foods. This stage was named Basket Maker I. The makers of the stone implements may represent people of Basket Maker I, or of an even older stage of culture. Be this as it may, the stone implements appear different from those in other recognized stages of Southwestern cultures.

Following these non-pottery people who lived on the river terraces, one recognizes sites covered with brown or red pottery fragments. These mark the home sites of the Sinagua. This brown or red pottery was manufactured by a method called "paddle-and-anvil." The potter built up her vessel out of coils of clay, laying one upon the other. Then, holding a mushroom-shaped anvil, usually of stone, on the inside of the vessel, she beat the outer surface with a wooden paddle, shaping the vessel to her taste. A favorite trick of the Sinagua potter, which she learned from her Mogollon neighbors of the White Mountains in Arizona, was to smudge the interior of bowls. After A.D. 1150, much of the Sinagua pottery had a good red surface in place of the earlier brown, and a highly polished metallic black interior. The black interior may have been produced by removing the bowl from the fire while still hot and inverting it on a bed of cedar bark or of pine needles, care being taken to cover the exterior with sand to prevent smudging it also.

Unlike the neighboring Kayenta Indians, who buried their dead in a flexed position, and the Hohokam, who cremated theirs, the

Fig. 13. Remains of an early earth lodge (A.D. 600 to 700) showing oval plan, slab walls, side entrance, fireplace on the left near center, and clay ridges on floor extending from fireplace to walls.

Sinagua buried their dead in an extended position and placed with them many offerings. These were often the most treasured possessions, as one can see from the burial of the great magician so fully described by Mc.Gregor (1943).

A.D. 500–700.   Archaeologists first recognized the Sinagua as living three hundred fifty to four hundred years before the eruption of Sunset Crater, when the people, very few in number, lived in earth lodges with entrances facing the east, like those of Navajo hogans. These houses had central firepits and since the clay floors were below ground level, they have been called pithouses. At this time not many neighboring tribes are distinguishable. The Kayenta branch to the north and east of the Sinagua, now called "Modified Basket Makers," lived beside the Little Colorado River and traded with the Sinagua

Fig. 14. One type of Cohonina earth lodge was a large wooden structure, 25 to 30 feet square, with a fireplace and a side entrance.

across fifteen miles of waterless desert. In the Salt River Valley, the
Hohokam villages were well established along their irrigation canals.
To the southeast the Mogollon, a mountain people, dwelt on both
sides of the Mogollon Rim around the White Mountains in Arizona
and New Mexico. At this time we can recognize only these four tribes,
but more intensive field work will probably show that other groups
lived to the west at this period of Sinagua history.

A.D. 700–900.   During the eighth and ninth centuries Sinagua culture remained much the same except for deeper pithouses, but the
population showed a definite increase. Although the Kayenta and
Mogollon remained in their old territories, the Hohokam from the
south moved into the Verde Valley, carrying with them their distinctive culture, including the idea of ball courts. A new tribe appeared in the territory northwest of the Sinagua, extending from the
San Francisco Mountains north to the Grand Canyon and west to the

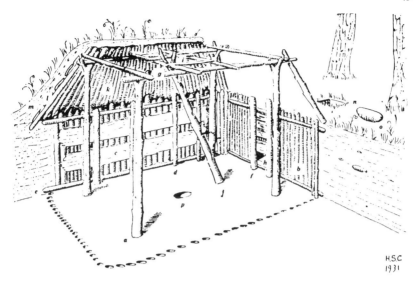

Fig. 15. The Sinagua built a deep pithouse lined with stone or wood. *a*, four posts supporting roof; *b, c, d, e,* and *f*, parts of side walls; *g*, roof beams; *h*, opening of ventilator; *i*, entrance hatchway; *j*, ladder; *k*, roof poles; *l*, pine bark; *m*, earth covering roof; *n*, exterior opening of ventilator; *o*, slab to cover opening of ventilator; *p*, fireplace.

edge of the plateau. We call this tribe the Cohonina. The Cohonina lived in shallower earth lodges, whose construction seems more haphazard. All these five tribes had a lively trade with one another.

A.D. 900–1060.   Still the Sinagua lived much as they had in the previous centuries. As in the previous four hundred years, the houses were located near permanent water holes such as Turkey Tanks, 18 miles east of Flagstaff, and on the alluvial slopes of the San Francisco Peaks within reach of a few springs.

The pithouses were deeper, and were entered, not through a ramped vestibule but by ladder through a square hole in the roof. Draft for the fireplace was provided by a horizontal flue through the wall at floor level. In the earlier houses this flue was connected

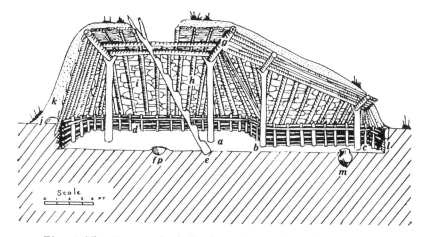

Fig. 16. The Sinagua also built alcove houses of wood. *a, b,* and *c,* posts supporting the roof; *d,* wooden walls; *e,* ladder; *fp,* fireplace; *g, h, i, j,* and *k,* parts of roof; *l,* stone at end of alcove; *m,* storage pot buried in alcove.

with another sloping up to the ground level more steeply than an entrance way. After 1070, the flue to the surface was vertical as in Kayenta kivas. The smoke from the fire escaped through the entrance hatch.

A.D. 1060–1125. About 1065, as we have seen, Sunset Crater deposited a layer of black ash over the Sinagua country. In a few years people flocked into this black sand area. This human influx brought new ideas, as well as new arts and crafts, to the Sinagua. The most notable of these new arrivals, the Hohokam from southern Arizona, settled near the present Winona Station (on the Santa Fe Railway), bringing with them their characteristic red-on-buff pottery, and their peculiar house-type, an earth lodge with a gable roof, which they duplicated in their new environment. Also, they built their familiar ball courts in the new territory. For a generation (1070 to 1100), they remained true to their original way of life, but later they seem to have been absorbed gradually into the life of their Sinagua neighbors.

A.D. 1125–1200.   Shortly after 1100, a new idea in housing spread across the land, an idea that had developed in New Mexico a hundred years earlier. Up to that time the Sinagua had lived in pit earth-lodges with perhaps an aboveground masonry building of tiny rooms in which they stored their harvests. Now the family enlarged one of the storage rooms and moved into it with the children. It was a much drier, more convenient, and more flexible house than the old earth lodge. Although the wave of cultural ideas affected the Kayenta in much the same way as the Sinagua, the Kayenta kept the old pithouse as a kiva. The Sinagua let the abandoned pithouse fall into ruins and become filled with trash.

The game courts introduced into the black sand area in the late eleventh century were probably still in use in the mid twelfth century. The court at Winona shows five periods of rebuilding.

Fig. 17. Ball court at Winona after excavation. It was 100 feet long and 45 feet wide, with sloping walls of dirt 9 feet high. The figure in the center is pointing to the center stone.

After the family came out of the ground and settled comfortably in their fine stone buildings with neatly plastered walls, their married daughters added rooms to the house and moved in with their families. This was the beginning of the growth of large apartment houses in which other families joined the original group for protection and convenience.

During the early part of the twelfth century people continued to live in the cliff dwellings at Walnut Canyon and under overhanging ledges in many other canyons. We do not have a clear idea of the exact time of the abandonment of these sites, but few if any lasted until 1200.

We have seen how the unit house grew into the pueblo during the early twelfth century. The pueblos continued to grow in size, but were fewer in number. By the thirteenth century only four pueblos seem to have been left near the San Francisco Peaks, and by 1325 all were in ruins. The last four pueblos we now know as Elden Pueblo, Turkey Hill, Old Caves, and Wupatki.

Elden Pueblo was excavated completely in 1926 by J. W. Fewkes and J. P. Harrington for the Smithsonian Institution. Although detailed notes were taken, no complete report has been published. Our knowledge of this site is contained in two short papers, one by Dr. Fewkes and the other by Walter Hough.

Elden Pueblo contained about forty-seven rooms. A small, rectangular, unroofed court with a banquette around three sides may have served as a place for ceremonies. Dr. Fewkes uncovered one hundred fifty burials with many artifacts, including pottery and ornaments. All the bodies were buried in an extended position. Not a single one was flexed. Most of the pottery belonged to the twelfth century, but there were types of later date, showing that the pueblo was not completely abandoned until early in the thirteenth century. Charcoal was found in one of the rooms but was not saved, because at that time Dr. Douglass had not discovered its possibilities for dating by dendrochronology.

In 1900 Wupatki Pueblo was visited by Dr. Fewkes, who at that

Fig. 18. Wupatki Pueblo from the west.

time saw material, now lost, that had been recovered by Ben Doney from the pueblo. In 1933–34 the site was partially excavated by the Museum of Northern Arizona and by the Civil Works Administration. The final report has not been published but several short papers have summarized the results.

With its three stories Wupatki was the largest pueblo of the black sand country, sheltering perhaps two hundred inhabitants. A unique feature of the ruin is the circular, and probably unroofed, amphitheater with a northeast entrance and an earthern banquette around the wall. There was no fireplace or ventilator.

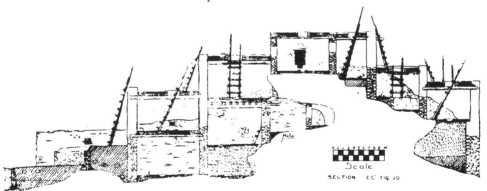

Fig. 19. Reconstructed section of Wupatki by Fisher Motz. The left side is east.

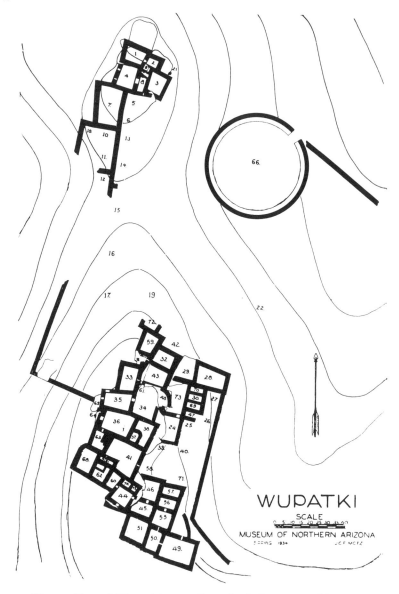

Fig. 20. Plan of Wupatki, a medium-sized Sinagua pueblo. It has been about one-third excavated by the Museum of Northern Arizona, in part with Federal funds under the Civil Works Administration.

A hundred yards north of Wupatki lies a well-preserved ball court of red sandstone. This masonry construction is unique in the San Francisco Mountains area, for all the other six known ball courts there have earth walls. This ball court has not yet been excavated. Therefore, we do not know whether it was contemporary with the pueblo or is the remnant of an earlier occupation of the region. Since contemporary ball courts have not been discovered near Turkey Hill, Elden, and Old Caves pueblos, one would infer that by 1200, at least, the game had died out.

Because of the dry climate, much timber suitable for dating has been preserved at Wupatki. The dates from this source indicate that many trees were cut in 1137 and that building, or at least replacement of timbers, went on until the early thirteenth century. Pottery has also given us a clue as to the time of occupation; we know that the site was occupied as early as 1050 and was abandoned before 1250.

The arid climate has also preserved many fragments of more perishable wooden and fabric materials from this pueblo. We know that the men wore breechclouts and carried burdens with a tumpline. A number of burials have supplied pottery and ornaments, so that we know more of the material culture of Wupatki than of any other contemporary site in the area.

The people of Wupatki buried their dead extended, often with the head toward the east. But the Kayenta people a few miles north buried their dead in a flexed position.

For the Sinagua we have very little evidence on disposal of the dead before 1070, when the use of cemeteries became common. Since a few burials of the early Sinagua have been stumbled upon, we presume that burials were made at random, away from dwellings.

Because the cemeteries of the later period are easily recognized, amateur archaeologists have dug in nearly all of them. Therefore, the number of skeletons recorded by trained archaeologists undoubtedly forms a very small percentage of the whole. The evidence that seems most significant in the record of burials is whether the body was "extended" (laid out horizontally) or "flexed" (bound up in a

Fig. 21. Wupatki. Amphitheater. A circular structure with banquette; similar to a Kayenta kiva, but seemingly was never roofed. It had a side entrance and no ventilator.

Fig. 22. The masonry ball court at Wupatki.

Fig. 23. Timbers from a collapsed roof in Wupatki show roof construction. Note original plaster on wall to the left.

sitting position), and how the skull was deformed. In the Sinagua culture most of the bodies were extended, and the back of the skull (the occipital region) was deformed. In the Kayenta culture, the body was flexed, and the skull was deformed in the lambdoid region.

In the spring of 1939, the Museum of Northern Arizona, in cooperation with the Works Progress Administration, partially excavated the Ridge Ruin, a medium-sized pueblo lying some twenty miles east of Flagstaff. In an abandoned pithouse near the ruin, the expedition discovered a burial which proved to be one of the richest in artifacts ever found in the Southwest. It was probably the tomb of a most important man.

A space about seven feet long and four feet wide had been excavated in the floor of an abandoned room. In this the body was placed, together with twenty-five pieces of pottery, an unknown number of baskets, and a mass of exquisite turquoise jewelry and ceremonial objects. More than four hundred arrows were scattered on the body. The tomb was roofed with juniper poles, and the whole structure was covered with earth. Of outstanding interest among the artifacts was a small cylindrical basket covered with more than fifteen hundred bits of turquoise as a background for a design in yellow made up of porcupines' incisor teeth. There were baskets coated with clay, which had then been painted in red, blue, and green with designs similar

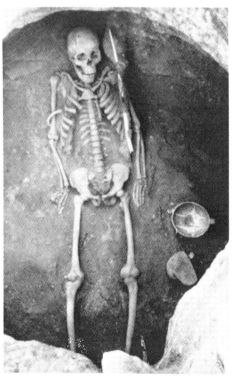 

Fig. 24a. Extended burial with offerings.   *Fig. 24b.* Flexed burial with offerings.

to those of the pottery. Some of the ceremonial wands were carved in the form of hands, while others represented the hoofs of deer, and some were encrusted with turquoise mosaic. A nose plug of red argillite with blue turquoise buttons on the end was found on the skull below the nose; turquoise earrings in the position of the ears, as well as other ornaments, show how greatly personal adornment was valued. The fine artistry and technical skill combined in these objects indicates the progress of these peoples' crafts.

Although no textiles were preserved after burial for seven hundred years in damp soil, yet textiles must have been there. We can visualize the kind by studying a contemporary burial in a dry cave in the Verde Valley which was uncovered several years ago by Clarence King. He found a blanket of cotton cloth, sized, and painted in black with a beautiful design common on Anasazi and Hohokam pottery. This is now a treasured object at the Arizona State Museum in Tucson.

A.D. 1200–1300.   In the thirteenth century, there was a marked drop in the population of the black sand area, with a corresponding increase in the Verde Valley. Elden, Wupatki, Walnut Canyon, Ridge Ruin, and hundreds of other sites were abandoned; only two pueblos, Turkey Hill and Old Caves, are recognized as persisting.

Turkey Hill, a site with about thirty-one ground-floor rooms, was excavated in 1927–28 by Dr. Byron Cummings for the University of Arizona. We know from tree-ring dates that it definitely existed from 1168 to 1278, and was abandoned before 1300.

Old Caves, a pueblo with about eighty ground-floor rooms, was visited by Dr. Fewkes in 1900. He made a reconnaissance, but did not excavate. No excavation was ever undertaken by trained investigators. The whole site has now been ruined by pot-hunters. We have no dated timbers but we do know from the potsherds that it was not completely abandoned until the last half of the thirteenth century and may even have been occupied for a few years into the fourteenth century.

Fig. 25. A reconstruction of the head of a Sinagua man buried at Ridge Ruin. This shows his bead cap, turquoise nose plug, and turquoise shell ornaments. *Reconstruction by Virgil Hubert.*

CHAPTER VII

Some Neighbors of the Sinagua

WHEN TRAVELERS visited the Southwest in the middle of the nineteenth century, they noticed evidences of a prehistoric civilization which seemed different from prehistoric cultures found in other parts of the United States. Since many of the best-preserved houses were built on ledges under overhanging canyon walls, these early white explorers called the houses "cliff dwellings." And because the ruins still so clearly showed the great skill of their long-dead builders, it was popularly believed that these "cliff dwellers" must have been related to the Aztecs of Mexico, whose advanced civilization had been made so well known by Prescott. Thus, all over the Southwest, we find prehistoric sites bearing such names as Montezuma's Castle and Aztec Fort.

Although the early scientific explorers knew that the remains they visited had not been left by the Aztecs, they did think of the cliff dwellers as a single, advanced Indian tribe. When in the early 1900's the ruins and artifacts from different parts of the Southwest were studied, it soon became evident that the "cliff dwellers" were merely prehistoric pueblo peoples and that those of one river valley had a slightly different way of life from those in another valley—so the divisions of pueblo culture were named from the valleys in which the ruins were found. Thus the archaeologists spoke of the people of the San Juan, the Little Colorado, the Gila, and the Rio Grande.

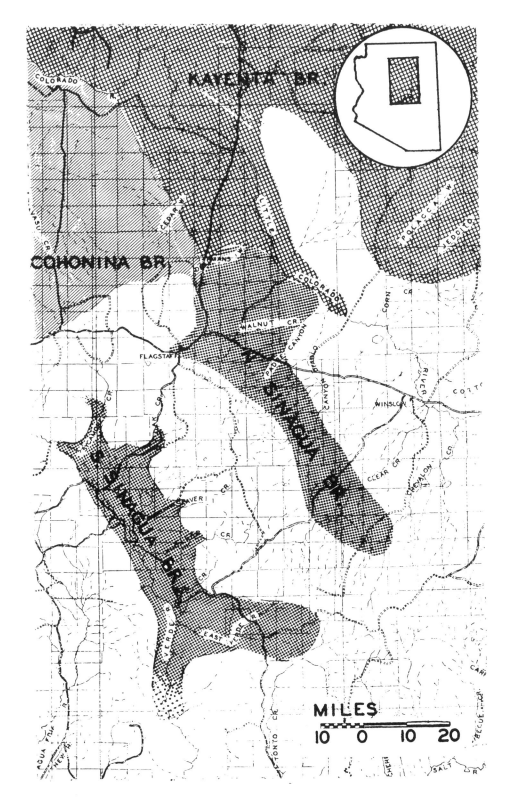

More intensive studies in the 1930's showed that the entire Southwest was occupied in prehistoric times by far more Indian tribes than the earlier works had ever dreamed. And further research revealed that the distribution of each was not necessarily confined to a single river system. In order to talk about these tribes and to study their relationships, H. S. Gladwin of Gila Pueblo at Globe, Arizona, suggested a nomenclature that had no strict geographical connotation. Even though there might be strong evidence that specific prehistoric tribes did exist, he suggested that we call them "branches," because the word has no inference of political organization.

Surrounding the Sinagua—the people of the black sand—we recognize five other tribes or branches: the Kayenta branch, named after an Indian trading store in Navajo country; the Cohonina branch, the Hopi name for the Havasupai Indians; the Prescott branch, from the city of Prescott; the Mogollon branch, named after the Mogollon Mountains in New Mexico; and the Hohokam, the name the Pima call their own ancient peoples. With these five branches, the Sinagua of the black sand had more or less intimate relationships at one time or another.

The various Indian "tribes" that surrounded the Sinagua on every side affected them, of course, in many ways—through trade, migration, and perhaps through war. Each branch maintained its integrity over a long period of years with frontiers sometimes static, but more often fluid, when one group expanded at the expense of another. By archaeological methods we can follow the fortunes of all five branches that surrounded the Sinagua.

THE KAYENTA. From the highest summit of the San Francisco Peaks, all the territories of the Sinaguas' neighbors can be seen. This commanding point gives a view to the northeast over the country once occupied by the Kayenta, the Indians who built the great cliff dwellings in the Tsegi Canyons—Kiet Siel and Betatakin. We can see on the dim horizon the rounded dome of Navajo Mountain near the

Fig. 26. A part of northern Arizona showing the relation of the areas occupied by the various prehistoric Indian tribes, dated about A.D. 1100.

Fig. 27. Kiet Siel. This Thirteenth Century pueblo is well preserved because it was built in a cave protected from moisture.

northern boundary of the Kayenta. About seventy miles away to the northeast are the mesas of the Hopi—the living descendants of the Kayenta. Archaeologists have traced the history of the Kayenta–Hopi Indians for over fifteen centuries. We know them first as primitive agriculturalists who made no pottery. Because baskets were the only containers they had for their harvest and for serving food, they are known as "Basket Makers." After this primitive beginning, we find the introduction of pottery making, and we can trace their architectural history from primitive pithouses to elaborate pueblos with underground ceremonial chambers called "kivas." These Indians artificially flattened the upper back of the skulls of their children, and, like their Hopi descendants, buried their dead in a flexed position.

After 1300, the territory of the Kayenta shrank from an area including most of northern Arizona to a small region surrounding the present Hopi mesas. However, it is not likely that the Hopi of today are pure-bred Kayentas. It is believed that after 1300 the Kayentas living on the Hopi mesas were joined by bands from other tribes, so the Hopi ancestry from the viewpoint of a geneticist is probably very much mixed.

The Kayenta branch or tribe had cultural relatives to the west in Utah and to the east in Colorado and New Mexico. These related Indian tribes, including the Kayenta, have been called, collectively, "Anasazi," a Navajo name for "ancient people"—although they were not ancestors of the Navajo. The Anasazi were among the few primitive peoples of the world who intentionally made gray or white pottery by baking the clay in a fire, free from oxygen.

These Indians were the originators of the masonry pueblo. Earlier, however, they lived in circular pithouses, reproduced in later times as the circular kivas of their pueblos. By means of trade the Anasazi exerted such influence on their neighbors that the pueblo way of living spread from a small area in New Mexico and southern Colorado eastward to beyond the Pecos, west to the Virgin, and south nearly to the present Mexican boundary.

THE COHONINA.   To the north and northwest of the San Francisco Mountains lies a rolling country, partly covered with pinyon and juniper trees and partly with grassy plains, extending to the great gash of the Grand Canyon. These lands from 700 to 1150 were the home of an Indian tribe which we have called the Cohonina. From the summit of the Peaks, one can trace their eastern boundary, marked by the edge of the forest west of the Little Colorado River, to the Grand Canyon, which formed the northern boundary of Cohonina territory. On the horizon is the row of hills that marked the western frontier. The pine forest at the northern base of the San Francisco Peaks was the southern edge of the Cohoninas' range.

The Museum of Northern Arizona has excavated a number of the houses of this tribe, and has uncovered many objects that illustrate the handicrafts of the people. The house of the Cohonina was variable. Sometimes a large earth lodge was associated with a small masonry structure of two or three rooms apparently used as a granary. Recently another house-type has been reported. This seems to have been a brush structure used only for sleeping, for it lacked a fireplace. Adjoining this shelter was an area of smoothed ground, covered by a shade supported on four or more posts. The presence here of a fireplace indicates that this shaded but open "room" was the center of domestic activity for the early Cohonina. After about the year 1000, when living near the frontier of the neighboring Sinagua, the Cohonina built masonry "forts" on easily defended hilltops.

Their thin, beautifully shaped storage and cooking vessels show that the Cohonina were excellent potters. A common type of manufacture was the paddle-and-anvil method, using a wooden paddle, and an anvil that was probably a water-worn pebble. In some cases, a potsherd-scraper was employed. Small pitchers in which the handle was attached to the rim are very common and distinguish the pottery of the Cohonina from that of other contemporary prehistoric tribes of Southwestern Indians. The Cohonina fired their pottery in an atmosphere free of oxygen as did the Kayenta, so that the color is quite consistently gray. That they admired red pottery can be seen, for, after the firing they gave many of their gray jars a wash of red ochre.

A large number of vessels of black-on-white pottery manufactured by the neighboring Kayenta tribe found their way to Cohonina sites, an indication of a lively trade back and forth across the Little Colorado River. Indeed, most of the wares in which the Cohonina served their food came from other peoples such as the Kayenta, just as we use English, French or German wares. The Cohonina themselves made but one decorated type and that only rarely.

The Cohonina had a characteristic long, triangular arrow point, and ground their corn on a metate, often closed at one end.

We know nothing about the physical type of the Cohonina for no burials of undisputed Cohonina origin have ever been found. We suspect that they cremated their dead and it would seem that they did not gather up the ashes, but let them lie wherever the cremation fire was built, for no urn burials have ever been located.

The earth-lodge sites of the Cohonina are common but not conspicuous. Because they are hard to see, amateur archaeologists usually fail to recognize them.

Nearly all we know of the nonperishable objects used by the Cohonina is derived from the discovery of Medicine Cave in 1927. This cave, eroded in the cinders under an old lava flow from a small volcano on the northeastern flanks of the San Francisco Peaks, proved on excavation to be a storage cave of the Cohonina. Since it was a dry cave, objects other than stone and bone were recovered, including five large perfect storage jars and other pottery objects. One jar, covered with a basket, contained about a peck of shelled corn. Some jars were covered with stone slabs and others with pieces of bark sealed with pinyon gum. A medicine man's outfit—a box made from the stem of a century plant—contained feather prayer offerings and polished pebbles. One small pottery jar held a tiny ball of fine cotton string wrapped in a corn husk. These interesting objects served to attract attention to the Cohonina branch and led to the excavation of more than fifty pithouses, some granaries, and two masonry forts.

Before A.D. 1000, the Cohonina must have led a comparatively peaceful life for they lived in isolated and defenseless earth lodges. But at times serious trouble must have threatened the pithouse dwellers, because we find near many of the centers of pithouse concentration, such as Medicine Valley, O'Leary Mesa, and about Williams, structures with thick masonry walls built on easily defended hills and ridges. These forts are contemporary with the pithouses and were obviously used for refuge in times of trouble. Typically, the forts are rectangular, but they were often adapted to the topography.

Since much of the archaeological field work described in this book centered in and about Medicine Valley and Bonito Park, we must not overlook the geographical importance of this area, for it forms one of the most accessible passes over the San Francisco Mountain

volcanic field from the Kayenta country to the Sinagua and Hohokam. This pass is called the Coconino Divide, altitude 7,200 feet.

A modern traveler, approaching this pass going north from Flagstaff on U.S. Highway 89, traverses the agricultural areas of Doney
and Black Bill parks and climbs through pine forests to the divide.
Here the road passes between the tall San Francisco Peaks, altitude
12,700 feet, on the west, and O'Leary Peak, 8,926 feet, on the east.
Then the road continues north, dropping down through beautiful
Medicine Valley to Deadmans Flat. Near the top of the pass a valley
opens out toward the east, with Sunset Crater and the Bonito Lava
Flow at the farther end. This basin, enclosed by O'Leary Peak on the
north and recent cinder cones on the east and south, is known as
Bonito Park.

The loose alluvial soil of the pass is formed as outwash fans from
the Pleistocene glaciers on the San Francisco Peaks, and was satis-
factory for primitive agriculture. From 900 to 1060, about one to two
hundred people lived in this immediate region—a relatively dense
population for those times. Since the pass formed the frontier between
several different prehistoric Indian groups, the archaeologist is not
surprised to find here evidences of considerable cultural mixing.

Although several other routes between southern and northern Arizona were available to these early people, the Coconino Divide marks
the shortest and easiest. Therefore, one might expect to find, and does,
the ruins of fortifications that were erected to guard the pass.

Medicine Fort on a slight rise west of Highway 89 at the head of
Medicine Valley is such a fort. Medicine Fort, excavated by a party
from the Museum of Northern Arizona in 1930, proved to be a
rectangular compound, 28 by 56 feet, and encompassed by walls
four feet thick and originally eight feet high. Following the inside of
the walls, a shelter supported on pine poles surrounded a court open
to the sky. Under these sheds about fifteen large storage jars had been
resting at the time the fort was destroyed by fire. Opening into the
court by a door was a series of small rooms which had been used as

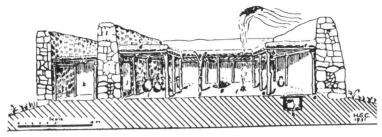

Fig. 28. Reconstruction of Medicine Fort, once used as a refuge by members of the Cohonina pithouse dwellers in times of stress. It might have been a trading store, as it lay in a mountain pass on a trail between northern and southern Arizona.

granaries. Since there was no sign of continuous occupation, it is believed that the people of the neighborhood retired to the fort only in time of danger. Their corn they stored in the granary, and their water in jars. Thus they were prepared for a siege.

Recent excavation of Cohonina sites suggests that many of the houses were not occupied the year around, but only in the summer. The winter homes have not yet been recognized.

About 1150 the Cohonina disappeared from the San Francisco Mountain region, although they continued to live in and around Havasupai Canyon. Recent work suggests that they were ancestors of the Havasupai Indians now living in the Grand Canyon.

Our knowledge of the Cohonina is based on the work of L. L. Hargrave, E. H. Spicer, J. C. Mc.Gregor, and D. Schwartz.

THE PRESCOTT. Looking southwest from Agassiz Peak of the San Francisco Mountains, one sees a fifty-mile belt of forest, ending in rough mountains. In the valleys of this country there dwelt, in prehistoric times, a tribe of Indians whom we call the Prescott branch. We know that in A.D. 900 they occupied an area extending west from Chino Valley to the Hualpai Mountains which, viewed from the San Francisco Peaks, form the western sky line. Although a few sites have been excavated, we know but little of the Prescott branch.

In the eleventh century, bands of this tribe had migrated north as far as Chino Valley, and in the 1100's there were a few families living on the northeast side of the San Francisco Peaks. Their life on the plateau after they left the region of the Aquarius Mountains seems to have been a slow migration toward the east and northeast.

Sites once occupied by this Prescott tribe can be recognized by the very characteristic pottery, which seems crude compared to that of the Kayenta, for the temper is coarse, with much mica, and the surface is unpolished. Parts of the same vessel may be red or yellow and other parts gray because it was fired in an uncontrolled atmosphere.

These Prescott Indians had a curious way of painting a decoration in black *inside* the necks of their large storage jars, many of which were grand affairs, sometimes three feet high. The ability to make such large jars does show that they had considerable technical ability.

In early times they lived in pithouses. They also built rectangular masonry forts on hilltops or other easily defended spots. After 1100, they adopted the house type of their neighbors, a masonry structure with contiguous rooms, which we would call a pueblo. They did not cremate their dead, but buried the bodies in an extended position. No Prescott sites are known that date after 1200.

The relationship of the Prescott tribe to their neighbors is not yet clear. Some archaeologists feel that the modern Yavapai Indians may be their descendants, for the Yavapai were living in the Prescott area in 1583, when the first white men arrived. If this is so, we have only to account for two hundred fifty years to close the gap in our knowledge of the tribe. If, on the other hand, the warlike Yavapai are descendants of the Colorado River people, the latter may have driven the Prescott people before them as they migrated toward the east. As one can see, the Prescott branch presents many problems and deserves much study before we can answer all the questions.

The little we know of the Prescott people is based on the work of Caywood and Spicer, and Richard Shutler.

THE HOHOKAM. Looking south from the mountain one can recognize the Black Mountains west of the Verde Valley and the Four Peaks, conspicuous landmarks which bound the Salt River Valley on the east.

In the tenth century, as I mentioned earlier, the Salt and Gila valleys were occupied by a people with a high culture called the Hohokam.

If we concentrate our attention on a Hohokam village—one of many, perhaps, on the site where Phoenix stands today—we would notice oval houses of wattle plastered with mud, and with gable roofs thatched with grass. These houses are scattered without plan among large mounds of refuse composed of broken pottery jars, sweepings from the houses, and ashes from the fireplaces. The mounds are large because the village had several hundred years of history behind it. We would see little of architectural interest in the village except perhaps a large oval ball court between the area occupied by the houses and the green irrigated fields of corn and cotton. The ball court, with a flat floor nearly a hundred feet long and forty or fifty feet wide, has sloping side walls nine or ten feet high. The ends are open, forming two narrow passages which give access to the court. Could we have visited this ball court on the day of a ceremony, we might have seen the inhabitants of the village perched like birds on the top of the wall watching a game in progress. The game might have been a variation of the stick-and-ball game of the Hopi or a variation of the Maya game called Pok-ta-pok, which was played by two teams with a solid rubber ball. (One such ball was found near Gila Bend, Arizona.) The ball could not be touched by the hands of the players but was bounced from head to elbow to buttocks. It was a dangerous game and men were often injured.

Many persons have contributed to our knowledge of the Hohokam, notably Jesse Walter Fewkes, Harold S. Gladwin, Emil W. Haury, Albert Schroeder, and Odd Halseth.

THE MOGOLLON. To the southeast of the San Francisco Mountains the eye travels across what appears to be an endless plain broken by a few flat-topped mesas and on clear days one can see on the sky line the serrated outline of the White Mountains of Arizona, two hundred miles away. Around the White Mountains and beyond, from A.D. 500 to 1100, lived a people that have been called the "Mogollon."

These people lived in villages of pithouses, often with a great circular ceremonial pithouse nearby. They manufactured a brown or red pottery which was constructed by a method called coiled-and-scraped. Mogollon villages were scattered over a vast area from north of the White Mountains south to the Mexican border.

Many archaeologists have excavated Mogollon villages: Dr. Paul Martin of the Chicago Natural History Museum, Dr. Emil Haury of the University of Arizona, Dr. Charles DiPeso of the Amerind Foundation, to name a few who have contributed most of our knowledge of the culture.

We have now circumscribed the Sinagua and named the principal branches or tribes that had contact with them: the Kayenta, Cohonina, Prescott, Hohokam, and Mogollon.

PREHISTORIC LANGUAGES
OF NORTHERN ARIZONA

You may ask what language these northern Arizona Indians spoke. This question is a difficult one for the archaeologist to answer because he cannot dig an unwritten language out of a trash mound or a burial pit. However, he can make some shrewd guesses. It is fairly certain that the Hopi Indians are the descendants of the Kayenta branch. Besides, the Hopi speak a language related to that of the present-day Ute and Paiute Indians, bands of whom are known to have occupied old abandoned Kayenta territory. It is very probable that the people of the Kayenta branch spoke archaic Hopi.

In ascribing a language to the Cohonina, the archaeologist has very little to go on. At the present state of our knowledge we would make a guess that they spoke a language related to that of the Indian tribes now living in the valley of the Colorado River. This group of languages is called Yuman.

As it is probable that the Zuñi Indians are the surviving descendants of the Mogollon branch, we might ascribe to the Mogollon an archaic Zuñi language. Several archaeologists believe that the Hohokam spoke a language akin to modern Piman, for there seems to be a nearly unbroken record joining the Pima with the Hohokam.

There is then some basis for ascribing specific languages to the Cohonina, Mogollon, and Hohokam, but the languages of the Prescott and Sinagua branches offer greater difficulties, and it is impossible even to make a good guess.

Because the frontiers separating the Sinagua from the Kayenta and Cohonina were so permanent and interfered so greatly with the exchange of ideas, whereas the boundary between the Sinagua and Hohokam, on the other hand, was fluid and encouraged such an exchange, it might be suggested that the Sinagua language was related to that of the Hohokam and thus to modern Piman. But since some Hopi traditions consider Sinagua pueblo ruins to be early Zuñi, other anthropologists might use a different approach and consider the Sinagua language related to the Zuñi.

The evidence for attributing a specific language to the Prescott branch rests on still weaker evidence. If the Prescott branch represents one of the great migrations of surplus population out of the Colorado River Valley, its language would probably have been Yuman.

The evidence relating the languages spoken in the Sinagua and Prescott branches to any living language is so weak that a cautious archaeologist must answer, "I don't know."

CHAPTER VIII

H
OW THE COLORADO RIVER
AFFECTED ARIZONA PREHISTORY

IT IS IMPOSSIBLE to understand the archaeology of western Arizona, and particularly the origins of the Cohonina and Prescott branches, without background knowledge of the geography and people of the Colorado River Valley below Boulder Dam. The Colorado River closely resembles the Nile in its geography. Both rise in well-watered highlands and flow long distances through deserts to the sea, receiving little or no water on their way. Both, until they were dammed, carried large burdens of silt and built extensive deltas at their mouths. Heavy floods in the late spring and early summer inundate their flood plains. Although the Nile flows north from the highlands of central Africa and the Colorado flows southwest from the Rocky Mountains of North America, their deltas are at almost the same latitude, that of the Nile 31°N, and of the Colorado 32°N. This fact gives them similar climates in their lower reaches. The annual precipitation at the deltas of both rivers is very low and the summers are intensely hot.

The densely inhabited valley of the Nile extends in a narrow strip for over eight hundred miles, the inhabited portion of the Colorado River Valley but three hundred. The peoples of both the Colorado and the Nile made use of the annual spring floods to produce abundant crops. Both starved when the annual flood did not take place.

The deserts bordering the valley of the Nile protected the inhabitants against invasion. Only from the Sudan and from the Mediterranean could their enemies approach them in numbers. The people of the Colorado River Valley were similarly protected from their enemies by extensive deserts.

When a group of people occupies a particularly favorable environment in which surplus food of the right kind is produced, the population will tend to increase in numbers, and will become relatively more dense than in the surrounding regions in which the conditions are less favorable. If the area is surrounded by deserts or mountains, the immediate neighbors will exert little influence, and enemies in numbers would have to traverse an exceedingly inhospitable region in order to threaten the inhabitants. This isolation, then, will afford security, give leisure for the development of arts and crafts, and assure the people a long tenure in their favored valley.

Thus, with the same geographical factors operating, one would naturally expect the two peoples to react to their environments in a somewhat similar way and to make progress in a similar direction. This, however, was not the case. Over a period of four thousand years the Nile Valley supported highly civilized communities while those of the Colorado remained, by comparison, quite backward.

Before the white man came, there lived in the valley of the Colorado River five or more Indian tribes, forming a group related in language, material culture, social customs and physical type. We call these tribes Yuman, because they spoke languages related to that of the Yuma tribe, which lives near the junction of the Gila River and the Colorado.

When the Spaniards met these Indians of the river, they were not impressed by their cultural level. They found that the men wore no clothes at all, while the women wore two aprons woven of willow bark, one in front and one behind; of course, the climate is usually very warm. The Spaniards were impressed, however, by the number of inhabitants, and by the amount of food that was raised, particularly in the delta area, where corn, squash, and beans were grown in great abundance. These were cultivated in fields which were annually flooded by the river, just as were the fields of the ancient Egyptians. The Yuma Indians lived in large earth lodges, the roofs of which were supported on four posts. They cremated their dead but did not gather up the ashes. They made pottery vessels for cooking and storage and also made good baskets and, since there are sometimes freezes in the river valley in the winter, they wove blankets of strips of rabbit skin. They had no boats but constructed for use on the river large rafts made of bundles of reeds, braced with cottonwood poles. For long journeys, a cooking fire was built on a layer of earth near the raft's stern. However, these Indians usually crossed the river on cottonwood logs or on bundles of reeds, which they straddled, paddling with their arms. To ferry small children across the river, they built large pottery bowls in which the child was placed and pushed ahead of a swimmer.

Although these tribes were isolated from other Indians by deserts fifty to one hundred miles wide, they nevertheless had contacts across these deserts by several routes.

Since the people lived mostly on the flood plains of the river, when the spring flood occurred and washed away their homes, they took refuge on the river terraces and waited for the river to fall. As soon as the water drained off their fields, they returned to plant corn, squash and beans, and to build new houses on the old sites. Therefore, each year, traces of their occupation were buried under a layer of river mud. The ancient Egyptians also left little record of their homes, but they did build, on the river terraces, elaborate tombs and temples in honor of their dead. The Colorado River people, on the other hand, cremated but did not bury their dead, and so left practically no trace of their occupation of the river terraces.

The life of the Colorado River people probably was not very different from life in the late stone age in Egypt seven thousand years ago. The Yumans did leave small fragments of broken pottery on the terraces above the water's reach and in the neighboring mountains. From these fragments archaeologists have pieced together bits of evidence showing that they traded with their neighbors in the Salt and Gila basins. These bits of traded pottery tell us that these people were living along the Colorado River fifteen hundred years ago.

When the Spaniards arrived in the sixteenth century, they found, occupying the corridors leading out of the Colorado River Valley, tribes related in language, culture and physical type to those of the valley. On the route to the California coast lived the Kamia of the Imperial Valley, and the Diegueño, centering around present-day San Diego. The corridor up the Gila was occupied by the strong Maricopa. The route up the Bill Williams Fork was occupied by the Western Yavapai; and the way east across the northern deserts and mountains, by the Hualpai. The eastern boundary of occupation by Yuman-speaking peoples in historic times has been the Little Colorado, which was reached by the Northeastern Yavapai and the Havasupai. From these observations one would conclude that the river people have repeatedly produced a surplus population which, being warlike, has found its way by migration to other regions and maintained itself there.

In general, the Cohonina, those neighbors of the Sinagua who were described earlier, have more characteristics in common with the people of the Colorado River Valley than with the pueblo people of the plateau. We have noted that the Cohonina dwelt in earth lodges which sometimes utilized four post supports. We know that they cultivated corn, beans, and squash. They seem to have disposed of their dead by cremation, but did not gather up and preserve the ashes. They made gray pottery, moulded and thinned with a paddle and anvil. They used three-quarter-grooved stone axes, trough-shaped metates of a distinctive type, with two-hand manos often grooved. Their arrows were of reed with hardwood foreshafts. They made baskets of twilled woven yucca leaves, and coiled baskets built on a two-rod and bundle foundation. Pottery, tubular pipes, jars, and bowls, and circular discs made of perforated sherds, have been found. They had dogs but no turkeys.

Thus it would seem, on an inspection of the data available, that the river people repeatedly produced more children than could find a living on the river flats and that some, when they grew up, were pushed out and had to seek a home in other regions. One can postulate periodic waves of migration over the various trails out of the river valley into the neighboring regions.

A working hypothesis can be formulated that will lead us to critical investigations. We know that the adoption of agriculture must have led to an increased food supply which in time would lead to overpopulation. Such a period of overpopulation might have occurred in a period between the beginning of the Christian Era and A.D. 500. We can imagine a large group of Indians passing up Bill Williams Fork and occupying the Colorado Plateau, where dry-farming was possible.

CHAPTER IX

P
EOPLE OF THE VERDE VALLEY

SOUTH AND WEST of the San Francisco Peaks lies a broad band of pine forest thirty to fifty miles wide which breaks away in a series of high cliffs to lower lands. To the south of this zone lies the Tonto Basin, drained by Tonto Creek and the east branch of the Verde River, and to the west lies the deep Verde Valley itself, once occupied by a great marshy playa. Through all these valleys flow perennial streams of clear water which ultimately find their way into the Salt River flowing by Phoenix. We know that these deep valleys and the neighboring foothills were occupied in prehistoric times, for pottery contemporary with the earliest made on the plateau has been discovered there.

In the old muddy playa that once occupied the Verde Valley, over twelve hundred feet of sandstone, interspersed with beds of limestone, was deposited. In the erosion of these beds, natural caves were produced, and, since some of the material is soft, prehistoric men hollowed out artificial caves and used them as dwelling places and for storage of agricultural products. As much of the valley floor lies between three thousand and four thousand feet of altitude, the climate is hot in the summer, and many of the desert plants such as creosote bush and mesquite cover the valley bottoms and the limestone hills.

On the cliffs and terraces overlooking the Verde and its major tributaries are a score of large pueblo ruins such as Tuzigoot, Bridgeport, and Clear Creek. And in countless natural and artificial caves are cliff dwellings, of which Montezuma Castle is the finest example, where perishable objects have been preserved.

Prehistoric irrigation canals can easily be traced along the river valleys. One near Montezuma Well has been preserved by travertine deposits. A salt mine, once worked by the prehistoric inhabitants of the valley, has preserved some curious records. Since the miners used no props, the roof of the tunnel frequently collapsed, burying the unfortunate Indian with his tools, his clothes, and his torches of cedar bark. His body was salted naturally and partly preserved. Until recently no organized attempt has been made to save the valuable archaeological remains in the Verde Valley. In the past not only the local inhabitants but also the winter visitors contributed to the destruction and the dispersion of the material so that the archaeologist has little to go on in reconstructing the history.

Bringing together the few facts based on archaeological surveys, we can see that there dwelt in the Verde Valley two peoples, one related to the Hohokam of the Salt River Valley, and the other to the Sinagua about Flagstaff. Following up the Verde Valley from the junction with the Salt, the Hohokam brought with them their ideas of irrigation, constructing canals and diverting water to their fields. They made characteristic Hohokam pottery and dwelt in Hohokam houses, and near the mouth of Clear Creek we can see the outlines of some of their ball courts.

The Hohokam probably lived in the Verde Valley longer than any other one people of whom we have evidence, but, because they lived in shallow pithouses, they left remains so insignificant beside the great pueblos and cliff dwellings of later date that few archaeologists have ever noticed them. A study of their own pottery and the pottery they received in trade, as well as the finding of a great ball court over two hundred feet long, makes us think that the Hohokam were in the valley as early as A.D. 500.

While the Hohokam were irrigating their fields beside the river, relatives of the Sinagua lived a few miles away in the foothills of the escarpment to the east, using dry-farming.

We can see in the Verde Valley the same trend as among the other prehistoric tribes of northern Arizona. The dry-farmers of the foothills who lived until about 1100 in earth lodges adopted certain traits of pueblo culture, building masonry dwellings in the open and in caves under the shelter of overhanging cliffs. After 1100, having become irrigation farmers, they drove out or absorbed the Hohokam.

The people of the Verde were great traders. In payment for salt and probably cotton textiles, in which they excelled, they received quantities of pottery from less-favored areas. They made no good pottery themselves but purchased the best made on the plateau. Small, easily transported forms of early Hopi pottery occur in such quantities that some archaeologists believe Hopi-type pottery was made in the Verde Valley. This is unlikely, because it was made of Hopi-country, not local, clays. Moreover, Hopi-style storage and cookery wares are absent.

The history of human occupation of the Verde Valley covers an almost unbroken period from before A.D. 500 until the present time. We find the Hohokam living along the river until about 1100, when they seem to have been absorbed by the Sinagua. Out of this fusion developed a culture combining pueblo architecture with irrigation agriculture. The Sinagua lived in the Verde until about 1400 when they seem to have vanished. In 1582 Espejo found the valley occupied by Indians who probably belonged to the Yavapai tribe, the same tribe the Americans found occupying the valley in the 1860's. Therefore, the history of the Verde includes the Hohokam, the Sinagua, the Yavapai, the Spanish and the Anglo–Americans.

We also have some scattered evidence of human occupation of the Verde Valley prior to 500. Sites with stone implements and no pottery have been discovered on the terraces beside both dry washes and flowing streams. One such site on Dry Creek near Sedona, excavated in 1949, gives us a partial, though very fragmentary, picture of the culture of the pre-pottery people. Scrapers and other implements, more or less similar to those found on the terraces of the Little Colorado, were accompanied by basin-type metates and round or oval manos. This type of milling apparatus persisted until about A.D. 700, when it was replaced by trough metates and rectangular manos that were operated with both hands. The pre-pottery sites have not yet been dated with certainty but they probably antedate the beginning of the Christian Era.

CHAPTER X

D RAWINGS ON ROCK

OVER THE PLATEAU, on faces of cliffs and on large boulders are thousands of drawings, pecked, engraved and painted on the rock. These drawings, although crude, have a certain artistic value, and some study has been made as to their significance.

Placing them in relation to their proper tribe (branch) and period of time has not been a very successful pastime. When we know that a certain tribe has occupied an area where these rock drawings are found, we can hazard a guess as to the makers. Very often the drawings are close to a habitation and this makes the correlation even closer. It is, however, rare when a time correlation can be inferred, for many sites near drawings have been occupied over a very long period.

Not only do the drawings occur near habitations, but very often large prominent rocks on an important trail leading by such a site are literally covered with "inscriptions."

Have these drawings any meaning? In the Painted Desert of northern Arizona, one mile south of Willow Springs and six miles west of Tuba City, near U.S. Highway 89, several large boulders of red sandstone have broken from a cliff and rolled into a valley. Several of these rocks bear drawings or petroglyphs which date from the late prehistoric to the recent period and are quite unlike the ancient rock drawings associated with pueblo ruins and cliff dwellings. Several

Fig. 29. One of the picture rocks at Willow Springs near Tuba City, Arizona. Each drawing represents a visit of a Hopi man, on his way to the salt deposit in the Grand Canyon, the symbol represents his clan.

Hopi Indians have noted that the petroglyphs are Hopi clan symbols, although they lie fifty miles northwest of Oraibi.

Though unable to identify all the drawings, our informants have recognized most of them. Depending upon the skill of the artist, different forms of the same symbol appear. At other times different symbols stand for the same clan. Thus it is that a member of the Hopi Cloud Clan, for instance, will draw a picture of a cloud, lightning, a frog, a tadpole, or any aquatic animal to record his clan. The apparently unrelated symbols for a given clan are explained in a clan legend. Where the same symbol is repeated with the same technique, we were told that this represented repeated visits by the same individual. Among these symbols that our Hopi informant recognized are those of two recently extinct clans. He suggested that the unrecognized symbols may also be those of extinct clans which are now forgotten.

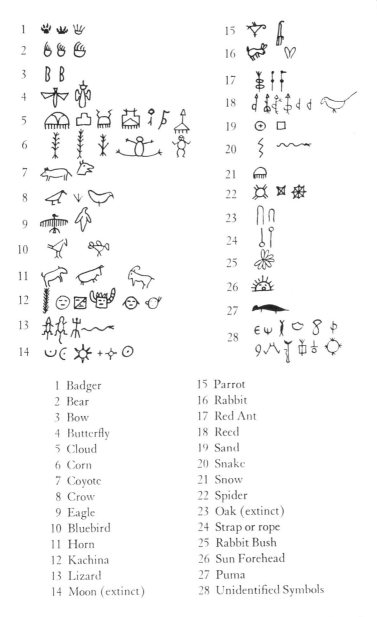

1 Badger
2 Bear
3 Bow
4 Butterfly
5 Cloud
6 Corn
7 Coyote
8 Crow
9 Eagle
10 Bluebird
11 Horn
12 Kachina
13 Lizard
14 Moon (extinct)

15 Parrot
16 Rabbit
17 Red Ant
18 Reed
19 Sand
20 Snake
21 Snow
22 Spider
23 Oak (extinct)
24 Strap or rope
25 Rabbit Bush
26 Sun Forehead
27 Puma
28 Unidentified Symbols

Fig. 30. Clan symbols near Willow Springs recognized by Edmund Nequatewa, a Hopi Indian.

A Hopi clan is an extended family in which the pedigrees are forgotten and which are traced through the mother to some mythical ancestor or group of migrants. Suppose you received your last name from your mother, not your father. Imagine a member, say of the Smith family, drawing on a rock a picture of an anvil. Another member might make a drawing of a hammer. If we knew the connection, we would know that both draftsmen belong to the same clan. A number of Hopi clans have died out recently in some of the pueblos because the female children died before they were able to reproduce.

The Hopi informant explained why his people left their "signatures" on the rock. He told how down in the depths of the Grand Canyon of the Colorado River and the connecting gloomy box canyon of the Little Colorado abide the spirits of departed Hopi. From the great canyon the Hopi emerged in the dim past and down into its mysterious depths the dead return. Legends deal with the ghostly inhabitants who, arising from the abyss with glowing eyes and monstrous form, travel out across the Painted Desert to revisit their earthly homes on the Hopi mesas, where they maintain a lively and beneficent interest in human affairs.

It is natural, therefore, that these great canyons, the abode of the dead, should be regarded with superstitious dread. In the bottom of the Grand Canyon, on the east side of the river below the junction of the Little Colorado, there is a salt deposit, formed by dripping springs in the canyon wall. An ancient trail runs from the Hopi villages across the mesas to the valley of the Moenkopi; then it follows the base of the Echo Cliffs to Willow Springs and thence turns west across the desert to the Little Colorado, which here lies in a deep canyon. Following down a tributary canyon to the Little Colorado, the trail leads along that river to the Colorado and thence to the Salt Spring.

From prehistoric times the ancient peoples have made this journey down to the salt mines, through the dreaded underworld. Only a man with a strong heart would dare go down out of his sunlit desert world into the eerie gloom of the canyon. Such a man would be proud to return alive and his desire would be great to have a permanent record of his adventure.

When the early salt gatherers trotted down the trail by the red Echo Cliffs, they felt a great urge to leave a record of their daring. They came upon a great sandstone boulder close beside the way and here they stopped and each man, with the point of a sharp rock, laboriously pecked into the smooth surface of the boulder the symbol of his clan, that all who saw it might know that they had passed that way. They may have been men of the Cloud clan or the Bear clan or, perhaps, a clan long since vanished and forgotten. But they set their marks, their record of a great deed.

Through the centuries many brave men came down the old trail upon the same errand, an unending line back into the dim past. Each man paused beside the boulder and placed his clan symbol beside those of his clan brothers who had preceded him. Finally, the great boulder became so crowded with an intricate record of the clans, an overlapping network which covered every surface of the rock, that they moved on to another boulder and then to another. Still they pass that way to the Salt Springs and leave their record on the rock (Colton and Colton, 1931).

Rock drawings have been recorded from many areas on the plateau. We have groups recorded by Guernsey and Kidder for the Kayenta branch in the Tsegi Canyons. The author has recorded hundreds in the Kayenta country near the Little Colorado at Crack-in-the-Rock, Picture Cave, Inscription Point, and other places. In the Sinagua area he has recorded them at Turkey Tank, Walnut Canyon, and Picture Canyon. Cohonina rock drawings are scarce.

Guernsey has shown that drawings of broad, square-shouldered men are characteristic of the Kayenta tribe before 800. Similar drawings of broad-shouldered men are also pecked in the rock in many places in the Little Colorado River Valley.

The Sinagua as a whole seem to have made more abstract designs than the Kayenta. The Kayenta living near the Sinagua frontier made more abstract designs than the Kayenta from "upcountry." Since

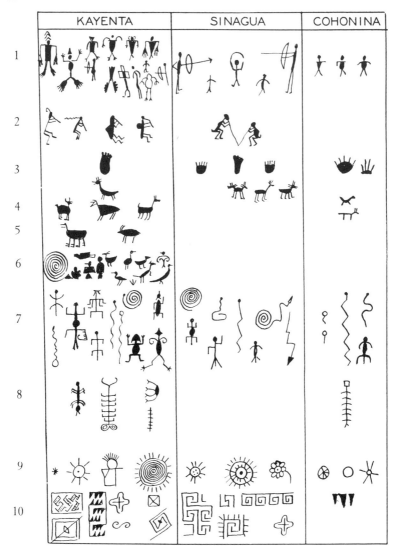

Fig. 31. Drawings from three different areas compared. The forms have been classified as: *1.* human, *2.* hump-back flute player, *3.* human or bear feet, *4.* deer, *5.* antelope, *6.* birds, *7.* reptiles and amphibia, *8.* centipedes, insects and spider, *9.* sun, and *10.* abstract drawings.

Fig. 32. Petroglyphs which seem to tell a story.

many of these designs were made near habitations, we might class them as "doodlings," drawings made to pass the time away. Since the Kayenta people in the Tsegi drew many mountain sheep and the Kayenta by the Little Colorado drew many antelope and birds, while the Sinagua of the San Francisco Mountains drew deer, it is probable that these drawings represent hunting fetishes, drawings made of the animal about to be hunted, so as to make the chase successful. Be this as it may, the Kayenta of the Tsegi lived in mountain sheep country; the Kayenta of the Little Colorado Valley, in antelope country; and the Sinagua, in deer country. Environment certainly had an influence on the drawings.

Since drawings of snakes, tadpoles, and other water animals are found about springs and water holes, we can infer that these drawings were also in the nature of fetishes.

The numerous drawings found at Inscription Point, across the Little Colorado from Wupatki, show many repetitions; so we conclude that these were signatures left by travelers along the trail, just as in later days the Hopi used the rock at Willow Springs.

The rock drawings of the plateau, then, were made for any of several reasons—as "doodling," as fetishes, or as travelers' signatures. Notwithstanding, some appear to tell a story, but this story may be the result of the visitor's imagination. Some symbols resemble those of European origin: the cross is fairly common, swastikas are not unknown, and with a little searching on some picture rocks one can find nearly all the letters of the Greek alphabet. I think we can say with confidence that the drawings do not represent any system of hieroglyphic writing. However, the drawings deserve much more study than has been given them and may in the future make more sense to us.

CHAPTER XI

COMMERCE IN ANCIENT TIMES

HISTORIC TIME in the Southwest begins about 1600, when permanent Spanish settlements were established in the Rio Grande Valley. In early Spanish documents we find references to Indian trade.

After the Pueblo uprising of 1680, when all the Spaniards were driven south to El Paso, Don Diego de Vargas was appointed governor of New Mexico by the viceroy. At that time a very important Mexican industry was the refining of silver ore, a process in which mercury was essential. The only source of mercury then was the red ore, cinnabar, mined in Spain; so the discovery of a red mercury ore in the New World would be of great economic importance. Some of the refugees from New Mexico in 1680 reported to the viceroy that a greasy red paint had been in common use at Santa Fe where the Spanish ladies used it for rouge. The viceroy therefore ordered de Vargas to procure all the information that he could about this red ore and its source. For this purpose de Vargas held an investigation at El Paso and, under oath, questioned a great many soldiers, friars, and others who had been in Santa Fe before the rebellion. From the reports of this investigation of 1691 we get our earliest references to Indian trade in New Mexico and Arizona.

De Vargas found that this very greasy red paint was in great demand by the Indians and that it was procured by the Hopi from a cave four days march west from their pueblos. De Vargas' famous entrada into New Mexico the next year was primarily a search for this cave, which he did not find. However, he did procure a burro load of the red ore from the Hopi. This he sent to Mexico City, where it was assayed and found to be iron ore, hematite, not cinnabar, the mercury ore they were seeking.

For the past three hundred years the Hopi have been buying this red paint from the Havasupai Indians, who live in a tributary of the Grand Canyon, four days by trail west of Oraibi. The Hopi buy it at $5 per pound and peddle it to other Indians at 25 cents a teaspoonful, thus making a tidy profit.

Although geologists know of a number of deposits of hematite in the Cambrian rocks of the Grand Canyon, the exact location of the Havasupai mine is not known, and the Havasupai are very tight lipped about its location.

Another business relation between the Havasupai and the Hopi is of long standing. The Hualpai Indians of northwestern Arizona have deer on their reservation. These they kill and skin. The hides they sell to their relatives, the Havasupai, in return for agricultural products or other goods. The Havasupai, having plenty of running water and much livestock, tan the skins with animal brains and trade the white hides to the Hopi for the latter's textiles and pottery. The Hopi are very industrious and manufacture the hides into white moccasin boots for their own women and for the women of the Rio Grande pueblos. In return, the people of the Rio Grande used to give the Hopi indigo, turquoise and jewelry.

Not only do the Hopi trade red paint to the Rio Grande but also garments woven by the men, including dresses for the women, belts, and ceremonial clothing for important Rio Grande burials. Up to 1910 or thereabouts, the Rio Grande pueblos, particularly Isleta, traded indigo from Mexico, which reached the Hopi in payment for their goods.

Trade is an exchange of goods and therefore we must call it business. When an archaeologist finds what he calls "intrusive" articles in a dig, articles that could not have come from the immediate neighborhood, he knows that the material was acquired either as loot from a raiding expedition, or through a business transaction. He knows that business transactions played a large part in the lives of the Southwestern Indians, and that trading expeditions were more common than those of war. The present-day Hopi, as well as other Pueblo Indians, are experienced traders, and frequently travel long distances alone or in groups. Father Garcés reported a Hopi and his wife two hundred miles from home trading with the Mojave Indians in 1776, and it was a common practice in the past for a group of traders to travel together for mutual protection. Even today the Hopi are notable travelers.

We also have evidence of extensive business relations among Indian tribes in prehistoric times. The Cohonina, who once occupied the lands now used by the Havasupai, had a village on the site of the present Supai village in the Grand Canyon. They therefore had access to the deposits of red ochre, the greasy face paint that is found in the Cambrian rocks near the bottom of the canyon. The Cohonina made use of this red paint, giving their beautiful large gray storage jars a coat of red ochre after firing.

It is interesting to note that at the prehistoric site in Supai, which was occupied from about 1000 to a little after 1100, there are found a large number of broken fragments of the small bowls made by the Kayenta to the east. This quantity of exotic pottery probably represents payment for red paint, for it is likely that this greasy red ochre was in demand as a face paint in those days even as now.

The Prescott tribe, near the present town of Chino Valley in Yavapai County, had a mine of a compact red shale that resembles the Middle Western pipestone. This shale was in great demand by the Sinagua and others for the manufacture of ornaments. It was used with turquoise in inlays, carved into shapes of birds, and ground into beads by the thousands. For this red "pipestone" the Prescott people seem to have received decorated pottery from the Kayenta, probably by way of the Sinagua.

The Verde Valley was a source of great natural resources for the people who lived there. From the region of the copper mines at Jerome they had malachite, which was valuable as paint and for ornaments. A prehistoric salt mine was worked near Camp Verde. The hot climate plus irrigation made it much easier to grow cotton than on the cold plateau where the Hopi had to develop a special variety. Very elaborate cotton textiles have come from caves in the neighborhood. All of these objects, beyond what they needed for their own use, they held for trade. Since these people of the Verde Valley did not make a good decorated pottery, they purchased their "table china"* from about 800 to 1300 from the Kayenta and other neighbors who made excellent black-on-white pottery. After 1300 they purchased their yellow "tableware" from the Hopi. The amount of foreign pottery in any region at a given time is a measure of business relations.

Most of the shell used in ornaments seems to have been gathered on the shores of the Gulf of California by the Hohokam and traded to the tribes of northern Arizona. A small amount, particularly abalone shell, came from the California coast. The amount of shell found from any period or area is another measure of trade activity. From Mexico by way of the Hohokam the Sinagua received copper bells and live macaws.

The Hohokam, having much to trade to the north, such as the copper bells, macaws, shells, and probably textiles the northern tribes lacked, never traded pottery there, for little or no Hohokam pottery is found on the plateau except at Winona in Coconino County, where a Hohokam colony was established about the year 1070. On the other hand, Kayenta pottery was traded to the Hohokam.

These are just a few of the many objects that were traded about prehistoric Arizona.

As you cast your eye over the Southwest, it becomes evident that pottery, particularly attractive small bowls and small jars, furnished an important medium of exchange. Even today at the Hopi First

---

* These Indians, of course, had no tables but served their food on the floor.

Mesa small decorated bowls and jars are manufactured in great volume and sold to the tourist through curio dealers all over the Southwest. In return the Indians procure groceries, salt, coffee and sugar. They therefore are able to have many things that they themselves cannot produce. It must be noted that only the small, easily transported objects are in demand for trade. The large bowls and jars rarely leave the mesa, or, when they do, are purchased by a few connoisseurs. The same was true in the past when great and often beautiful storage jars seldom left the tribe which produced them. These objects were too hard to transport and the danger of breakage was too great. The small, attractive, well-decorated pottery vessels had a wide appeal and could be transported easily by a man on foot, for these Indians, you must remember, had no beasts of burden. Tribes with abundant natural resources did not enter the pottery trade, while those without other resources were active in the manufacture of pottery, especially for trade.

Thus the Kayenta and their descendants, the Hopi, seem to have been the principal tribe in northern Arizona making pottery for trade. Although other tribes made good pottery, little of it left home. The Cohonina, for instance, made no pottery for trade purposes. Their large, beautiful jars and bowls were manufactured for home use only. Other people who had natural resources, such as the Sinagua of the Verde Valley, the Prescott people, and the Cohonina, did not manufacture decorated pottery for trade. The best decorated pottery seems to have been manufactured to trade for objects which the people desired and which they themselves could not produce.

The northern Sinagua who occupied the black sand area present an economic problem. What did they exchange for pottery from the Kayenta, salt and textiles from the Verde Valley, pipestone from the Prescott branch, turquoise from New Mexico, shell from Sonora and California, and copper bells from Mexico? If we list their natural resources we find they had little or no advantage over their neighbors. Their climate was cool, the agricultural possibilities adequate for subsistence farms, they had game; but their volcanic country offered no material that could be used in trade, except perhaps obsidian for arrow heads. Were the Sinagua manufacturers or were they tradesmen? Were the painted baskets a specialty of their own or were they made somewhere else? These questions we cannot answer yet. They pose intriguing problems for future archaeologists.

Since objects of one kind and another have been traded about the Southwest for the past fifteen hundred years, it will be interesting to present what information we have on the routes followed in this trade. In 1938 Dr. Donald Brand outlined a number of trade routes across Arizona, basing his work on the study of marine shells excavated from prehistoric sites. Some of the mollusks which produced the shells are known to live only in the Gulf of Mexico, others only in the Gulf of California, and still others only on the California Pacific Coast. From these data, he postulated a series of trade routes. To the information furnished by the shells we can add information derived from the distribution of traded pottery, the distribution of water holes, topography, and aboriginal trade routes of the historic period. With these additional data before us, we can locate the prehistoric trade routes in northern Arizona with considerable accuracy.

One main trade route east from the Pacific Coast crossed northern Arizona, and over it shell went east and pueblo pottery went west. This route followed generally the present U.S. Highway 66, lying a little to the north of it most of the way. This route branched near Peach Springs—one branch going northeast, following the rim of the Grand Canyon to the Moenkopi Valley, which it followed into Anasazi country; the other branch passed through the black sand country, followed up the Little Colorado and its tributaries into the Zuñi country and New Mexico. A route from the Gulf of California passed through the dense Hohokam centers about the present Phoenix, following up the Verde River, where the trail forked in the neighborhood of Camp Verde. One branch passed up Oak Creek to the region of Flagstaff, then north to the Moenkopi, which it followed into Anasazi country. The other branch went east from the Verde, following in general the route of the dry Beaver Creek, past Pine

Springs to Chavez Pass, then on to the Winslow settlements and the Hopi country. Over this trail quantities of Hopi pottery passed south into the Verde Valley, and shell, salt, and cotton textiles presumably went north to the Hopi mesas.

Another trade route of great importance left the Hohokam settlements about Phoenix, followed up the Salt River and its tributaries to Fort Apache and over the divide west of the White Mountains into the Little Colorado Basin to the Zuñi or Hopi country.

Over the Hopi–Verde trail we can imagine a Hopi traveler trudging along, a pack on his back suspended with a tumpline across his forehead. He is on his way from the Hopi country with a load of twenty or more small yellow bowls, six to eight inches in diameter, each with an attractive design in black. On the trail in the pine forest he passes another man, a Sinagua from the Verde Valley, trotting north, a bundle on his back. In the pack of the man from the Verde are rolls of textiles, each tied up in a neat bundle; a cotton bag, much darned, full of salt; a bag of buckskin containing a hundred olivella shells drilled for stringing, and half a dozen glycymeris shell bracelets wrapped in raw cotton.

Commerce has always been an activity among the Indians of the Southwest, past and present. The finding of foreign objects by an archaeologist is among the most exciting incidents of his work. The archaeologist cannot help but speculate on where the objects came from and how they got there.

CHAPTER XII

T

HE PREHISTORIC FARMER

THE PRESENCE or absence of prehistoric sites in the Southwest depends on the possibilities of agriculture. A study of the distribution of these sites in northern Arizona shows that dense populations existed only where light alluvial soil forms the surface cover or where a heavy clay soil is protected with a layer of sand. Irrigation by living streams was practiced only in the Verde Valley and below a few large springs elsewhere.

To understand the dry-farming methods used by the prehistoric inhabitants it is necessary to observe the agricultural methods of the Hopi Indians, who today use tools somewhat similar to those found in archaeological excavations. The principal implements employed are a hoe and a wooden digging stick. The Hopi now practice four types of agriculture, depending on the topography of the area to be cultivated. About springs the women terrace the hillside and plant small gardens in which they grow special plants, such as onions and peppers, that they can irrigate from the spring. Frequently a man dams a small wash. When sufficient alluvial soil has collected back of the dam he plants small plots of corn and beans. The larger fields are of two kinds. On alluvial fans crops are planted and irrigated after summer thundershowers by flood water led to the fields by a ditch; or crops are grown on the valley bottoms. In the Hopi country the soil is a hard-pressed sandy loam. Capillary action carries the underground

Fig. 33. A Hopi field watered by flood water from an arroyo.

moisture rapidly to the surface, where it evaporates, leaving a white scum of alkali, so that little water is available for plants unless they are deep rooted, like the salt bush. However, over some parts of the area low sand dunes travel slowly across the sandy loam, covering the soil with a sandy layer a foot or so deep. Because this dune sand is not hard packed, the water is not carried to the surface by capillary action and so the moisture is preserved in the loam below.

The seeds are planted with a digging stick, which may be thought of as a plow and drill combined, while the hoe is used in controlling weeds and in cultivating. The digging stick is a very useful and important tool and is much more valuable than a plow in the Hopi country because the plow disturbs such a large volume of soil that it makes the field subject to excessive wind erosion. This is an important matter because after the crops are planted in April or May come the windiest months of the year, May and June. Plowed fields often literally blow away.

Fig. 34. Hopi corn plant, showing the ears of corn growing close to the ground.

Fig. 35. Brush lines to hold the sand in a Hopi field.

Seeds planted with the digging stick disturb a very small area of the field and so do not aid wind erosion. To use a digging stick, which is about thirty inches long and flattened at the lower end, the Hopi kneels on the ground, grasping the stick with both hands about six inches below the upper end. With it he scrapes out a narrow trench about a foot long and three inches wide. He digs until he reaches moist soil, which may be as deep as one foot. Into the bottom of the deepest part of the trench he drops about twelve corn grains. Later in the season he pulls up the weakest plants, leaving only three or four in each hill to mature.

A layer of sand covering a compact soil forms a mulch, which keeps the underlying soil moist. Clay soils derived from the weathering of basalt or of limestone, as in the San Francisco Mountains, dry out very quickly and become nearly as hard as concrete. They cannot be broken with a stone hoe or a wooden digging stick. If moist, such soil can be cultivated easily with these tools.

To make use of sand-dune agriculture, the ancestors of the Hopi developed a special variety of corn with the distance between the higher roots and the lowest leaves sometimes as much as eighteen inches. In ordinary maize this distance is only about three or four inches. This greater length makes it possible to plant the grain in soil

Fig. 36. Lines of stones in a Hopi field.

covered with more than a foot of sand. To hold the sand cover, if the wind is blowing it away, the Hopi build lines of small brush held in place by stones. These lines are planned perpendicularly to the direction of the prevailing southwesterly wind.

We think it likely that the prehistoric inhabitants of the black sand area also practiced sand-dune agriculture, after the eruption of Sunset Crater, when the whole countryside was covered with a layer of black volcanic ash. We can see the lines of stones that supported the brush to hold the black sand cover. These lines of stone are most commonly found where the ash cover was thinnest, near the edge of the ash fall area, where it first began to blow away.

Fig. 37. A prehistoric digging stick which is similar to a modern Hopi digging stick. Approximately 20 inches long.

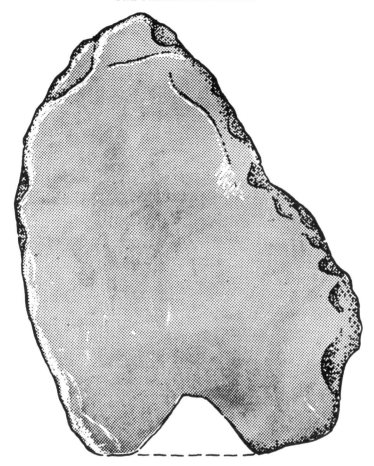

Fig. 38. Prehistoric hoe.

Close to many pueblos such as Citadel and Ridge Ruin, we find hillsides terraced with masonry walls and the terraces filled with trash from the houses. These terraces strongly suggest garden plots, but final proof is lacking. On the alluvial fans of the San Francisco Mountains we also find evidence of arroyo irrigation where rows of stones placed across draws probably represent dams to hold soil and indicate the sites of little gardens.

It is a general rule that the prehistoric dry-farmers of northern Arizona sought out areas with light alluvial soils or sandy plots for their fields. In subsistence farming the fields of each family need not have been large, for it was unnecessary to grow more food than the family could use in one year. Many gardens outlined by stones cover less than a sixteenth of an acre and compare in size with many Hopi garden plots of today.

It has been mentioned that the agricultural tools of the Hopi are a digging stick and a hoe, both of wood. Their Kayenta ancestors also used a wooden digging stick but the hoe was made of stone, probably hafted. The Sinagua of the black sand also used these same tools, but the hoe was apparently not hafted. It was made of a triangular piece of thin basalt, and after the fall of ash from Sunset Crater they made similar hoes of relatively soft Moenkopi sandstone. Such hoes are very abundant—eleven were found in one cache in the ash fall area. Such soft stone hoes could be used only in loosely packed sand and have not been found in any other region.

Fig. 39. A Hopi corn plant. Note the mesocotyl, the distance from roots to the lowest leaf. In Hopi corn this is very long and allows deep planting. *(After Collins).*

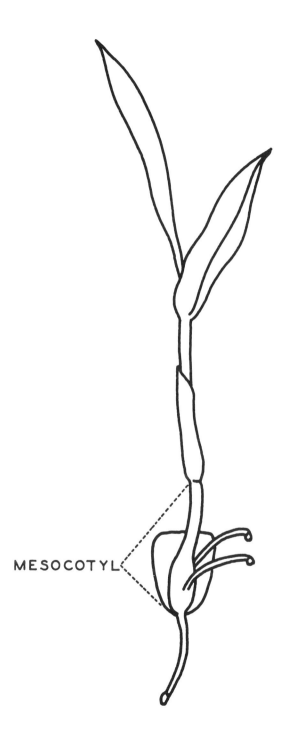

MESOCOTYL

CHAPTER XIII

P OPULATION
OF EARLY NORTHERN ARIZONA

IN 1950 about ten thousand persons lived in the area between the Little Colorado River and the San Francisco Peaks, including the city of Flagstaff and encompassing 42 townships, each of 36 square miles, making a total of 1,512 square miles or almost half a million acres. These people, mostly concentrated in the neighborhood of Flagstaff, derived their living from timber harvests in the Coconino National Forest, from tourists traversing two national highways, from Indian trading, and from livestock and agriculture. If we eliminate all of these groups that had no economic counterpart in the pre-Columbian past, we find that in 1950 there were fewer than one hundred persons on eighty farms or ranches who derived their principal living from the soil, mostly growing beans (Colton, 1949).

But the merest novice in the Southwest can see that the country once supported a great aboriginal population. Ruins everywhere testify to this conclusion. But when the white man came, the country appeared almost uninhabited, except for a few small areas. To the east of the Rio Grande ranged the Apaches, who may or may not have crossed the river at that time. Up the Chama River, a tributary of the Rio Grande northwest of Santa Fe, the elemental Navajo are said to have tended their fields of corn. The Yavapai, Hualpai, Mojave, Maricopa, and other Yuman tribes roamed the area between the Colorado and the Salt rivers. Spanish travelers rarely mention meeting, in the area between the Rio Grande and the Little Colorado, Indians other than the Pueblos: Hopi, Zuñi, Acoma, and Rio Grande.

A decline in population since prehistoric times is doubted by very few persons. Let us see what evidence exists for such a decline. To procure accurate figures is of course impossible, but from estimates we can see, at least in a relative way, what happened. We will start by examining the population of the black sand area because here we have the most data. To arrive at an estimate of the population of the black sand area at different dates, we consult the archaeological survey for the number and approximate size of sites, and for the pottery complex. With these data before us, by logical reasoning we can translate archaeological facts into terms of the number of people.

As the first step in the process we place together all the sites that have similar pottery complexes or, as the author has called them, "Ceramic Groups" (Colton, 1946). We have seen how stratigraphic studies show the order in which one pottery complex follows another. The dendrochronologist, having dated timbers from a number of small sites with similar complexes, can date the ceramic groups. Pottery, therefore, is used for correlation just as the geologist uses fossils. The changes that took place in decorative elements on the pottery from decade to decade indicate changes in time. Styles of pottery in the Southwest in prehistoric times were very much like those of women's clothing today. When a style is evolved in Paris, in two months it will have reached Hollywood. In another month the girls of Tokyo will adopt it. The progress of pottery styles was similar. From some center, a woman created an attractive design on her pottery. This was copied by others, and soon this design spread over much of the Southwest. Like modern women, the women of the Kayenta tribe, for instance, copied the styles of design from New Mexico, or from the Salt River Valley in Arizona, putting them on their own local pottery. They adopted the styles of decoration but did not adopt the foreign methods of manufacture; that is to say, they continued to use their own local kind of clay, moulding process, paint or temper, and firing method. Since attractive pottery types were widely traded and the styles of decoration frequently copied, it is possible approximately to date every prehistoric ruin in northern Arizona by the broken pottery picked up on the surface of the ground. Therefore, in our archaeological survey, when we record a site, the pottery fragments will furnish a rough date.

Up to a little after A.D. 1100 in northern Arizona, single families lived in earth lodges, which were usually pithouses. That is, the floor was below the level of the ground. Where timber was plentiful and stone poor, as in the San Francisco Mountains, timber was used for the retaining wall. In other places, the people laid up walls of masonry, sometimes well made and sometimes not. The roof was of timbers covered with brush and earth.

A decade or two after 1100, the people changed to masonry structures with flat roofs in which several families dwelt in contiguous rooms. This development marked a change from rural conditions to urban, a change from a family or a small group of families living in detached one-room houses placed near their farm plots, to many families living in multistoried apartment houses and walking some distance to reach their fields. I want to stress the fact that the change occurred in northern Arizona about A.D. 1120. The statement may not apply to the area east of the Chinle Valley or to New Mexico or Colorado.

So far we are on pretty firm ground, but now our toes will begin to leave the concrete, for we will have to make assumptions, and assumptions are dangerous. We must determine, 1) the number of rooms per site, 2) the number of families per room, and 3) the number of persons in a family.

In the pithouse period we find in the San Francisco Mountains area about three houses or dwelling rooms per site. In the pueblo period, after 1120, we can often count the rooms or, if we cannot, at least we can measure the area of the site and divide by the area of one room (180 square feet). Of course, the actual number can be determined only by complete excavation of the site.

In no area have we recorded all the sites, so that the calculations of the number of rooms are underestimates, rather than overestimates. On the other hand, pithouse sites are harder to locate than are the pueblo sites. Since the former are seldom visible from a distance, one has to be literally on top of the site to recognize it. Mounds or piles of conspicuous rocks mark the pueblo site and can be seen from a greater distance. Therefore, we record relatively more pueblo sites than pithouse sites. This difference may be balanced somewhat by multiplying the number of known pithouse sites by two.

The number of families to a room in the pithouse period we assume to be one. In the latter part of the pithouse period we find brush or masonry granaries of from one to four very small rooms associated with the pithouses. As they were not dwelling rooms, we do not count these in our estimates.

In the pueblo period we assume two ground-floor rooms for each family. This factor was derived by counting the ground-floor rooms in the Hopi pueblo plans made in 1881-82 by Mendeleff and comparing them with the 1890 Hopi census for each village. In 1890 the Hopi were living much as they had in prehistoric times, and the 1890 census was one of the best. The count gives 1,088 ground-floor rooms occupied by 1,996 Hopi, or nearly two persons per ground-floor room. As most pueblos are multistoried, this leaves plenty of extra space for store rooms.

If a population is more than holding its own, the number of persons in a family should be about five. Sauer (1935), in his study of Azatlan, places the number at six per family. Brainard (1935) shows that among the Hopi, a tribe that is little more than holding its own, the family averages 4.17 persons. From 1890 to 1930 the Hopi increased from 1,996 to 2,475, for a net gain of about 12 persons per year.

Although in an expanding population the number of persons per family—mother, father and children—must exceed five, I have selected four as the number occupying a pithouse and assumed that two persons occupied each ground-floor room of a pueblo.

TABLE I

INCREASE AND DECREASE OF POPULATION, A.D. 500–1400

Range of Dates	Median Date	Total Rooms	Total Families	Total Persons	% Loss or Gain Per Year
500–700	600	60	60	300	
700–900	800	76	76	380	.13% gain
900–1050	975	175	175	875	.74% gain
1050–1120	1085	941	941	3764	2.74% gain
1120–1200	1160	4208	2104	8416	1.64% gain
1200–1300	1250	306	153	612	8.70% loss
1300–1400	1350	0	0	0	1.00% loss

An inspection of Table I shows that a slow gain in population up to the time of the eruption of Sunset Crater in 1065 was followed by a very rapid gain, and then, after 1200, by an even more rapid loss.

We can see that the population slowly increased for four hundred years until, sometime after the year 900, it had reached about eight hundred seventy-five in number.

Then suddenly, within a single century, the population more than quadrupled, and again, in the succeeding 75 years, doubled again, making a total, about A.D. 1160, of almost ten times as many people in the area as had been living there less than two hundred years earlier.

After about 1200, the population began to shrink as dramatically as it had grown before, until by 1350 there were only about forty people left, all living in one small pueblo.

The story behind all this we have already outlined. The population had a normal increase; then, after the eruption of Sunset Crater, it increased not by normal reproduction, but because other people moved into the area. Can we explain the later decrease as easily? Yes and no. We know there was an exodus about 1300 into the Verde Valley, but the decrease began earlier—before 1200. Perhaps a population study of some other area will help fill out the story.

Another region where we have much information is Dogoszhi Biko, a canyon tributary to the Tsegi Canyons in northern Arizona.

A study of the population table of this area shows a rise in population from about twenty-five persons in the year 600 to about seven hundred in the year 1000. This rise was followed by a decline to a minimum of about one hundred sixty people around 1225. This severe decline Hack (1942) explained as caused by arroyo cutting, which lowered the ground water and destroyed the fields. The next 50 years, to 1275, showed a great increase in population to about nine hundred people or more because the arroyos filled and the ground water rose nearer the surface, making agriculture possible once more. A second cycle of arroyo cutting during the great drought caused the people to move away so that by 1300 the canyon was abandoned.

In the Hopi country we have another story: a slow increase until A.D. 1250, then a rapid increase to 1400, then a decrease. The fourfold increase between 1250 and 1400 might be explained by the migration of some of the people of the black sand, of Dogoszhi Biko, and of other areas, to the Hopi country. To see if such migrations are the true explanation, we made a study of the material supplied by the archaeological survey for all northern Arizona.

In the foregoing pages we have tested a few local areas and found that there was a considerable variation in their population curves, due to local conditions. Perhaps a study of a wider area will furnish us with a more general picture of what was going on in northern Arizona in prehistoric times.

Let us see how a broader archaeological survey throws light on the problem. The Museum of Northern Arizona has continued the survey of prehistoric sites begun by the author in 1916. Over five thousand sites are now recorded in our files. To simplify the study we will not consider here the whole of northern Arizona, but will select an area bounded on the north by Utah, on the west by the Colorado River and the San Francisco Mountains, on the south by the Little Colorado and the Puerco, and on the east by the Chinle Valley. Over most of this area the sites recorded are but a random sample of the sites present.

When making an archaeological survey, one soon discovers that sites in one area are much denser than in others. A five-hundred-square-mile area northeast of Flagstaff has been uniformly well explored. In some sections there are more than fifty sites per square mile and in others we have searched for hours without finding one.

It has been discovered that the reasons for the relative absence of sites in certain areas are ecological conditions such as little rainfall, poor soil, or lack of water for household purposes. In other regions where sandy conditions exist along valley bottoms, evidences of a relatively dense population were found, but the back country, away from the wash, was almost free of sites. Observing all these conditions, one is able to form an estimate of the number of sites at a given period and thus the population per square mile. If an area showed a population density of less than .05 per square mile, it was reported as "zero." Most areas show less than one person per square mile—he must have been pretty lonely—but some few small areas show a density of 30 per square mile.

Using the experience of this well-studied area, it is possible to divide all northern Arizona into areas of different estimated population densities at different dates. From these estimates we have plotted on the map the estimated number of persons per square mile for each of the periods of time we have considered. The sums of these populations are given in Table II.

TABLE II

PUEBLO POPULATION OF NORTHERN ARIZONA
BETWEEN 110TH AND 112TH MERIDIANS

A.D.	600	3,000
	800	10,000
	1000	23,000
	1150	19,000
	1400	7,400
	1890	2,000
	1950	4,000

We have by this means plotted the Pueblo population of northern Arizona north of the Santa Fe railroad and east of the San Francisco Mountains for each period from A.D. 600 to the present time. The population appears to rise from about 3,000 in 600 to about 23,000 in 1000, then to fall to about 2,000 by 1890. The Pueblo Indian population, i.e., that of the Hopi, has risen lately to about 4,000. The non-Pueblo peoples, such as the Navajo, are not included for they did not enter northern Arizona until the eighteenth century.

In comparing this table with the previous one we see that the local variations are wiped out and that there appears to be a simple maximum in the eleventh century, the climax of the pithouse period.

If to the number of Hopi living in this part of northern Arizona in 1930 is added the Navajo population of the same area and year, we discover the interesting fact that this region supports today approximately the same number of Indians as it did at the population peak of the eleventh century. However, this fact loses some of its significance when we realize that the more populous group of the twentieth century—the Navajo—are not primarily agriculturists. Their dependence on sheep, goats, and cattle results in economic use of more land than was possible for the prehistoric Pueblo peoples, whose only domestic animals were the dog and the turkey.

CHAPTER XIV

EMIGRANTS AND IMMIGRANTS

WHEN ALL our data on prehistoric population have been summed up, we can see that the population as a whole rose and fell. Several explanations have been advanced to explain the decline of prehistoric pueblo population. Archaeologists have almost invariably believed that the Pueblos diminished because of the inroads of nomads, such as the historic Ute, Navajo, and Apache. Other researchers, particularly dendrochronologists, believe that droughts caused death from starvation or migrations to better-watered regions. Physiologists point out that an increasing population would so destroy the game that the people would be reduced to a corn diet lacking in necessary vitamins. This would of necessity lead to deficiency diseases. Physiographers see the farming areas cut by arroyos, with resulting lower water tables. Indeed, as many different reasons have been given for the decline of Pueblo populations as for the decline of classic Greek civilization.

That people migrated in and out of the black sand area is evident from a study of the tables in the previous chapter. Although war and disease may explain a fall in population, a sudden rise, on the other hand, can be explained only by immigration. Memories of such movements of people comprise a large part of Hopi clan legends, and we have many evidences that such migrations really occurred although not necessarily exactly as the Hopi tell of them.

From about 600, when our population estimates begin, until about 1150, the number of people of northern Arizona increased slowly through natural reproduction. During this period only one migration seems evident. The population table of the black sand area indicates a great increase after the eruption of Sunset Crater which resulted in the area east of Flagstaff becoming one of the most densely populated farming communities of prehistoric Arizona.

The tables show a loss of population in most cases after 1100. Between 1200 and 1250, however, people flocked into the Tsegi Canyons, building many large pueblos like Betatakin and Kiet Siel.

The period between 1275 and 1300 seems to have been a particularly critical time for the people of the plateau. Northern Arizona, with the exception of the Hopi region, was abandoned as far south as the forested area north of the Mogollon and Tonto rims. During this period the Hopi country and Verde Valley received a great increment of population. Douglass (1935) through a study of tree rings has suggested a twenty-four-year drought at this time. Geologists (Hack, 1942) have presented clear evidence that an epicycle of arroyo cutting destroyed much of the best arable land. But since there are few arroyos in the Sinagua country, arroyo cutting could not have caused the migration of the Sinagua into the Verde Valley. Here we have another factor. The surface of the black sand was, after 1070, continuously disturbed by agriculture. By 1275 the sand may have been collected by wind into dunes and blown into canyons, exposing large areas of the old limestone or lava soil. This was as unsuitable for agriculture then as it is today.

While the regions about Navajo Mountain, the Tsegi Canyons, much of Black Mesa, and the Moenkopi drainage were being depopulated, the Hopi pueblos of Oraibi, Old Shungopovi, Old Mishongnovi, Old Walpi, Chuckovi, Hoyapi, Sikiatki, as well as other pueblos in the Hopi area, show an active building period. The same is true of the five great Hopi Pueblos in the Jeddito Valley—Kokopnyama, Nepshoptanga, Chakpahu, Kiwaiku, and Awatobi—which flourished with a total population of well over three thousand people.

From our population studies of northern Arizona we can see that people must have moved to and fro in the Tsegi area, in the black sand region, and in the Hopi country, but these local movements had no effect on the total population because they occurred within the boundaries of northern Arizona. If we are to account for the decrease of Pueblo population by emigration, we must try to see what happened during the period of population decline between 1150 and 1600 when we have evidence that many persons moved from northern Arizona to some more favored region. If we consider each prehistoric tribe, one by one, we find that the Kayenta, Cohonina, and Prescott branches dwindled away, the Kayenta alone leaving modern descendants—the Hopi. There is no evidence that any large number from these three branches moved out of northern Arizona. Some of the Sinagua, on the other hand, did migrate to the Verde Valley, but these left no permanent population increase in their new locality. The few Sinagua that emigrated were a very small proportion of the northern Arizona population.

There is also some evidence that the Sinagua in the Verde Valley traveled on south to the Salt River Valley. Other Indians from the White Mountains seem to have traveled east and joined the Zuñi. And at this time a number of the large Hopi and Jeddito pueblos were abandoned.

It is perfectly obvious that emigration took place, but it played a minor part in the disappearance of the prehistoric Pueblo Indians of northern Arizona. We must seek some other cause.

In a study of all these separate areas from 1150 to the coming of the Spaniards, we may observe a certain trend—from more and smaller pueblos to fewer and larger. If we could have visited northern Arizona in 1150, we would have seen hundreds of small masonry pueblos scattered on both sides of every valley everywhere, with a large total population. Three hundred years later we would have found the whole population compressed into about twelve large villages. Although each of these large pueblos held fifty times as many people as a little pueblo of the 1100's, yet the total population of the area was probably not one-quarter as great.

CHAPTER XV

URBAN LIFE
IN EARLY ARIZONA

IT IS CERTAIN that warlike nomads hovered on the borders of the Pueblo area. Luzan in 1582 mentions them, but there is no documentary evidence that the Navajo or Apache were much of a threat to the Pueblos before they received horses. Indeed, it has not been demonstrated beyond a doubt that the Apache and Navajo were in Arizona at all before 1700. The nomads mentioned by Luzan were more probably Yavapai, Ute, or Paiute. Moreover, we may doubt that, in a semiarid region, nomadic hunters without horses or other beasts of burden seriously troubled a dense sedentary population. It was only when the population dwindled that the raiders' inroads became important.

Haury has shown that droughts were sometimes so severe that a considerable number of people migrated to new homes looking for water. Droughts no doubt led to starvation, disease, migration, and wars, but droughts were probably, in the long run, not much worse in the years after 1100 than in the eight hundred years that preceded. Although tree ring studies show that the rainfall was increasing between 600 and 1000, there was no correlation between rainfall and population after 1000. As we have seen, the big decline in population began long before the great twenty-four-year drought that ended in 1300, although this drought has been considered the major catastrophe in Pueblo history.

Prehistoric Indians were doubtless subject to deficiency diseases, but probably not much more so than at present. Anyone who is familiar with the diet of the Hopi realizes that the Pueblo Indians make use of many wild plants. They have many kinds of "spinach" which they gather locally or cultivate in a small way. They also sprout beans in their kivas in the winter. Even without the animal viscera they eat, they would have a considerable variety of vitamins. Therefore, lack of vitamins from animal sources could hardly be a serious factor in causing deficiency diseases.

The physiographers have shown us that arroyo cutting such as we see today all over the plateau has taken place in recurring cycles with periods of arroyo filling between. Some of these cycles have been dated and correspond to crises in plateau history when people moved about and certain areas were abandoned (Hack, 1942). This factor could not have been important in the black sand region because there are few if any arroyos to be affected, although over the plateau as a whole, arroyo cutting furnishes an important explanation for the loss of population and must not be cast aside.

There are other local causes for the abandonment of certain areas. There is little doubt that the large Winslow pueblos were abandoned by the prehistoric inhabitants when their irrigation water carried alkali to the fields, just as happened between 1876 and 1889 in the same area when the Mormons, who founded Brigham City and Sunset, had to abandon their homes.

For the total abandonment of much of northern Arizona we must look for causes more general than local. We see that the population rose while the people lived in pit earth lodges and fell when the pueblo became their home. An explanation of this is suggested when we study the lives of the present-day Hopi and Navajo.

Here we have two peoples living in the same environment. But the "urban" Hopi are little more than holding their own in population, while the pastoral, rural Navajo are increasing at a rapid rate. The Navajo live in earth lodges very similar to the early Kayenta, Sinagua, and Cohonina of the era called Pueblo II. It seems reasonable that the Navajo now occupying the same area and living under much the same conditions as the pithouse people before 1100 would furnish us with contemporary material with which to study the conditions of life of the prehistoric pithouse dwellers. The main observable difference is that the Navajo are mostly pastoral whereas the pithouse people were primarily agricultural. But in certain fundamental conditions of life they are alike. The Navajo earth lodges, called "hogans," are usually widely spaced, and it is rare that one finds as many as four of them close together. The Navajo move seasonally to summer and winter residences as do many other people in the United States (albeit for different reasons). Therefore, their water is not contaminated by human excreta, since their supply is usually far distant from their living quarters. Although human excreta are deposited not far from the hogan, they do not present a menace to health because of the sparsity of population and the semiarid climate.

Like the pithouse dwellers of yore, the Navajo are increasing rapidly. Since 1868, when they were replaced on the reservation after their forced sojourn at Bosque Redondo, their number has increased, it is said, from 8,000 to over 70,000. I think the 8,000 figure is far too low a value, as information exists that Colonel Kit Carson did not capture more than half of the tribe while the rest scattered to the Rainbow Plateau, to Black Mesa, and into the Little Colorado River Valley. We should consider 16,000 a much more likely figure. Even then the increase is phenomenal, for in sixty years they have increased threefold, for an average gain of about 3% per year. In the 1820's and 1830's, when the population of the United States was largely rural and immigration was at a low ebb, the annual national increase was a little more than 3%. In the four centuries from 600 to 1000 the pithouse people increased at an average rate of 1–2% per year. The Hopi have been increasing about .5% per year in modern times.

The Hopi family, on the other hand, lives in crowded quarters. Families live close together, and the excreta are often deposited in the narrow plazas, streets, middens, and passages near the houses. Were it not for the arid climate, living conditions would be impossible.

Although the drinking water is usually procured from a spring at some distance from the village, yet in times of heavy rainfall, temporary pools filled by surface runoff form on the rocks close to the village. This water is contaminated with excreta. Rain water happens to be of ceremonial importance. When one protests to a Hopi grandmother about giving an infant a drink from the pool in the street, she will tell you that the water can't be bad because it fell from the clouds and so was especially sent by Sotuknangu, the Heavenly God. The mortality of Hopi children under two years of age is very great, especially after the summer rainy season. I have no exact figures (the Indian Bureau before 1938 kept no detailed vital statistics), but in 1934 very many of the children under the age of two years died of infantile dysentery at Shungopovi and at First Mesa.

I want to stress this difference between the sanitary conditions of families who live in independent houses and the conditions under which people live in city "slums." There is a good deal of evidence that the people of cities, until very recently, did not reproduce themselves, and had it not been for immigrants from the country, the population of cities would have dwindled. If this applies to cities in so-called civilized countries, why would it not also be true of the Hopi? They are living under conditions little better than those of a European city two hundred years ago, as pictured by Lowie (1929). Indeed, as late as 1890, when the author visited German cities along the Rhine, where sewage flowed in the streets, he found them more odiferous than any Hopi town. It is only by modern disposal of sewage and sanitation that modern cities hold their own. In Philadelphia in my youth, the annual loss of life of adults by typhoid fever and of children by infantile dysentery was a disgrace. I can remember the headlines in the papers when the annual September typhoid epidemic was reported. All statistics show that from the point of view of population increase it is better to live in a farmhouse in the country than in a city flat.

It is evident that the decline in the early population of northern Arizona is a very complex affair and that local conditions had im-

Fig. 40. The Salt Bush Zone (altitude 3,500 to 5,500 feet) is so dry and hot that the few habitations of prehistoric people lie near the permanent streams where they could practice irrigation.

portant results. In one place nomads may have burned a pueblo; in another place arroyo cutting may have destroyed the fields; and in another area the springs, where drinking water was procured, may have dried up. Failure of summer rains may have destroyed the crops in one place or another. And one factor that would affect all the pueblos is bad sanitation, which, although not the complete answer, is a very important and neglected factor.

Fig. 41. The Juniper Zone (altitude 5,500 to 7,000 feet) furnishes the best climatic conditions for agriculture with ample time between frosts, and in some years there is sufficient rainfall for dry farming.

Fig. 42. The Yellow Pine Zone (altitude 7,000 to 8,000 feet) marks the upper limit of agriculture. In many years there are too few days between frosts for corn to mature.

CHAPTER XVI

CONCLUSION

WE HAVE PRESENTED an outline of evidence on which the archaeological story of northern Arizona is based. We have followed that story from the earliest evidence of primitive hunters who lived on the terraces beside the Little Colorado River. We have traced the history of several Indian tribes over a millennium. We have noted their relationships and followed their rise and fall.

A local event of great importance not only to the inhabitants of the San Francisco Mountains region but to other more distant peoples was the eruption of Sunset Crater. As from a pebble dropped into a pond, waves spread out, affecting the population of a wide area. We have seen how the volcanic ash of this eruption made agriculture exceptional in a place where it had been nearly impossible before. We have seen a prehistoric land rush into the area, with immigrant farmers arriving to cultivate the new land. We have visions of the original peaceful inhabitants resisting this invasion but later absorbing the newcomers.

As conditions became peaceful once more we found groups of pit-house people living in scattered farmhouses without any thought of defense. About 1125, the inhabitants moved their living quarters out of the pithouse into the masonry granary. Among the Sinagua, when the old pithouse was abandoned as a living place it did not remain as a kiva, as it did in the Kayenta tribe. The little stone farmhouses of two or three masonry rooms, occupied by a single family, dotted the landscape. The daughter, when she married now, did not need to leave her mother's house. She simply added a room or two for her family. We also think that sometimes unrelated families joined the house group, adding more rooms. So began the pueblo, which grew until it was the home of many families.

The continual cultivation of the black sand cover brought to the surface the finer ash particles and exposed them to the wind, so that the black sand that had preserved the moisture in the soil was gathered into dunes. In some places, the sand was now so deep that the digging stick could not reach the underlying soil. In others, the corn planted in the deep sand would fail to reach the surface. In still others, the black sand cover was entirely removed and the soil dried out, destroying the crops. The families who lived in the small stone houses began to join with other families in large masonry apartment houses to protect themselves against their neighbors. When the people crowded together the sanitary conditions became increasingly bad, causing the death of many young children from "summer complaint." The population dwindled until by 1275 but two large apartment houses were occupied, and by not more than six hundred people. The drought which followed (1275-99) caused these last inhabitants to move away to join other groups who dwelt by the Little Colorado River at Winslow or at Chavez Pass or in the Verde Valley. By 1300 the cycle of development initiated by the eruption of Sunset Crater was complete. It was a cycle unique in American history.

For the next six centuries, the country about the San Francisco Peaks held no permanent population. The Hopi visited it for timber and medicines. The Yavapai from the Verde Valley and the Havasupai from the Grand Canyon hunted in the area. But until Flagstaff was settled in 1882, on the completion of the Atlantic and Pacific Railway, now the main line of the Santa Fe Railway, no permanent population lived in the region of the black sand.

We must think of the inhabitants of the black sand region as people who had problems of population, food and sanitation to meet.

They engaged in business and had economic relationships with neighboring tribes. They formed a microcosm, a small world in itself, and so had to meet in one way or another most of the problems that we have to meet today. Perhaps a study of their history will help us meet some of our own problems of urbanization and avoid some of the mistakes made by earlier inhabitants.

Fig. 43. The Douglas Fir Zone in northern Arizona (altitude 8,000 to 10,000 feet). In this region the nights are too cool and the season too short for agriculture, but the area was used by the prehistoric inhabitants as a hunting ground.

BIBLIOGRAPHY

Bancroft, H. H.
  1888   *History of Arizona and New Mexico*. New York.
Bartlett, Katharine
  1934   "The Material Culture of Pueblo II in the San Francisco Mountains, Arizona." Museum of Northern Arizona, *Bulletin*, No. 7.
Blom, Frans
  1932   "The Maya Ball Game Pok-da-pok." Tulane University, *Middle American Research Papers*, No. 5, 485–526.
Brainard, Margaret
  1935   *The Hopi Indian Family*. University of Chicago, thesis.
Colton, Mary-Russell F., and Harold S.
  1918   "The Little-Known Small House Ruins in the Coconino Forest." American Anthropological Association, *Memoirs*, IV, No. 4.
  1931   "Petroglyphs, the Story of a Great Adventure." *American Anthropologist*, XXXIII, No. 1, 32.
Colton, Harold S.
  1918   "The Geography of Certain Ruins near the San Francisco Mountains, Arizona." Geographical Society of Philadelphia, *Bulletin*, XVI, No. 2.
  1920   "Did the So-Called Cliff Dwellers of Central Arizona also Build 'Hogans'?" *American Anthropologist*, new series, XXII, No. 3, 289–301.
  1929   "Sunset Crater and the Lava Beds." Museum of Northern Arizona, *Museum Notes*, II, No. 4.
  1929   "Walnut Canyon." Museum of Northern Arizona, *Museum Notes*, II, No. 3.
  1930   "The Citadel." Museum of Northern Arizona, *Museum Notes*, II, No. 8.

1931 "Archaeological Survey of the Museum of Northern Arizona." Museum of Northern Arizona, *Museum Notes*, IV, No. 1.

1932 "Survey of Prehistoric Sites in the Region of Flagstaff, Arizona." Bureau of American Ethnology, *Bulletins*, No. 104.

1932 "Walnut Canyon National Monument." Museum of Northern Arizona, *Museum Notes*, IV, No. 11.

1932 "Sunset Crater; the Effect of a Volcanic Eruption on an Ancient Pueblo People." *Geographical Review*, October, 582–90.

1933 "Pueblo II in the San Francisco Mountains, Arizona." Museum of Northern Arizona, *Bulletin*, No. 4, 3.

1933 "Wupatki, the Tall House." Museum of Northern Arizona, *Museum Notes*, V, No. 11.

1935 "Discovery of a Large Oval 'Bowl' at Flagstaff." *Science*, LXXXII, No. 2132, 9.

1936 "Rise and Fall of the Prehistoric Population of Northern Arizona." *Science*, LXXXIV, No. 2181, 377–43.

1938 "Names of Four Culture Roots in the Southwest." *Science*, LXXXVII, No. 2268, 551–52.

1938 "Economic Geography of the Winona Phase." *Southwestern Lore*, III, No. 4.

1946 "The Sinagua." Museum of Northern Arizona, *Bulletin*, No. 22.

1949 "Prehistoric Population of the Flagstaff Area." *Plateau*, XXII, No. 2, October.

Colton, Harold S., and Hargrave, Lyndon L.

1937 "Handbook of Northern Arizona Pottery Wares." Museum of Northern Arizona, *Bulletin*, No. 11.

Caywood, L. R.

1935 "Tuzigoot; the Excavation and Repair of a Ruin in the Verde Valley near Clarkdale, Arizona." *Southwestern Monuments*, May, 249.

Caywood, L. R., and Spicer, E. H.

1936 "Two Pueblo Ruins in West-Central Arizona." University of Arizona, *Social Science Bulletin*, No. 40.

Collins, G. N.

1913 "A Drought-Resisting Adaptation in the Seedlings of Hopi Maize." *Journal of Agricultural Research*, I, No. 4, 293.

Cummings, Byron

1904 "Ancient Inhabitants of the San Juan Valley." Utah University, *Bulletin*, No. 3, 2.

1916 "Kivas of San Juan Drainage." *American Anthropologist*, new series, XVII, 272.

1930   "Turkey Hill Ruin." Museum of Northern Arizona, *Museum Notes*, II, No. 11, 6.

Douglass, A. E.

1919   "Climatic Cycles and Tree Growth." Carnegie Institution of Washington, *Publications*, No. 289.

1929   "Secret of the Southwest Solved by Talkative Tree Rings." *National Geographic*, December.

1935   "Dating Pueblo Bonito and Other Ruins of the Southwest." National Geographic Society, *Technical Papers, Pueblo Bonito Series*, No. 1.

Espinosa, J. K.

1934   "The Legend of Sierra Azul." *New Mexico Historical Review*, IX, 113.

Fewkes, J. W.

1895   "Archaeological Expedition in Arizona in 1895." Bureau of American Ethnology, *Seventeenth Annual Report*, Pt. 2, 519.

1900   "Pueblo Ruins near Flagstaff, Arizona." *American Anthropologist*, new series, II.

1904   "Two Summers Work in Pueblo Ruins." Bureau of American Ethnology, *Twenty-second Annual Report*.

1906   "Antiquities of the Upper Verde River and Walnut Creek, Arizona." Bureau of American Ethnology, *Twenty-eighth Annual Report*.

1926   "Archaeological Studies in the Wupatki National Monument." Smithsonian Institution, *Miscellaneous Collections*, LXXVIII, No. 1, 96.

1926   "Archaeological Field Work in Arizona, 1926: Elden." Smithsonian Institution, *Miscellaneous Collections*, LXXVIII, No. 7, 207.

Forde, C. D.

1931   "Ethnography of the Yuma Indians." University of California, *American Archaeology and Ethnology*, XXVIII, 83–278.

Gladwin, W., and H. S.

1930   "Western Range of the Red-on-Buff Culture." Gila Pueblo, *Medallion Papers*, No. 5.

1930   "Archaeological Survey of the Verde Valley." Gila Pueblo, *Medallion Papers*, No. 6.

Gladwin, H. S.

1934   "A Method for the Designation of Cultures and Their Variations." Gila Pueblo, *Medallion Papers*, No. 15.

Gladwin, H. S., Haury, E. W., Sayles, E. B., and Gladwin, N.

1937   "Snaketown." Gila Pueblo, *Medallion Papers*, No. 25.

Gregory, H. E.

1916   "The Navajo Country." U.S. Geological Survey, *Water Supply Papers*, No. 380.

Guernsey, S. J.
1931   "Exploration in Northeastern Arizona." Harvard University, *Papers of the Peabody Museum of American Archaeology and Ethnology*, XII, No. 1.

Guernsey, S. J., and Kidder, A. V.
1921   "Basket Maker Caves of Northeastern Arizona." Harvard University, *Papers of the Peabody Museum of American Archaeology and Ethnology*, VIII, No. 2.

Hack, J. T.
1942   "The Changing Physical Environment of the Hopi Indians of Arizona." Harvard University, *Papers of the Peabody Museum of American Archaeology and Ethnology*, XXV, No. 1.

Hargrave, L. L.
1929   "Elden Pueblo." Museum of Northern Arizona, *Museum Notes*, II, No. 5.

1930   "Shungopovi." Museum of Northern Arizona, *Museum Notes*, II, No. 10.

1930   "Prehistoric Earth Lodges of the San Francisco Mountains." Museum of Northern Arizona, *Museum Notes*, III, No. 5.

1931   "First Mesa." Museum of Northern Arizona, *Museum Notes*, III, No. 9.

1932   "Oraibi; Brief History of the Oldest Inhabited Town in the United States." Museum of Northern Arizona, *Museum Notes*, IV, No. 7.

1932   "Guide to Forty Pottery Types from the Hopi Country and the San Francisco Mountains, Arizona." Museum of Northern Arizona, *Bulletin*, No. 1.

1933   "Pueblo II Houses of the San Francisco Mountains, Arizona." Museum of Northern Arizona, *Bulletin*, No. 4.

1935   *Report on Archaeological Reconnaissance in the Rainbow Plateau of Northern Arizona and Southern Utah*. Berkeley.

1938   "The Results of a Study of the Cohonina Branch of the Patayan Culture." Museum of Northern Arizona, *Museum Notes*, XI, No. 6, 43.

Hargrave, L. L., and Haury, E. W.
1931   "Recently Dated Pueblo Ruins in Arizona." Smithsonian Institution, *Miscellaneous Collections*, LXXXII, No. 11.

Haury, E. W.
1934   "The Canyon Creek Ruin." Gila Pueblo, *Medallion Papers*, No. 14.

1936   "The Mogollon Culture in Southwestern New Mexico." Gila Pueblo, *Medallion Papers*, No. 20.

Haury, E. W., and Hargrave, L. L.

1931 "Recently Dated Pueblo Ruins in Arizona." Smithsonian Institution, *Miscellaneous Collections*, LXXXII, No. 11.

Hough, Walter

1919 "Exploration of a Pit House Village at Zuñi, New Mexico." U.S. National Museum, *Proceedings*, LV, 409–31.

1923 "Pit Dwellings and Square Kivas, San Francisco River." *El Palacio*, XV, No. 1, 3–9.

1932 "Decorative Designs on Elden Puéblo Pottery, Flagstaff, Arizona." U.S. National Museum, *Proceedings*, LXXXI, Article 7, 1–11.

Huntington, E.

1914 "Climatic Factors in North America." Carnegie Institution of Washington, *Publications*, No. 192.

Judd, N. M.

1930 "Excavations and Repair of Betatakin." U.S. National Museum, *Proceedings*, LXXVII.

Kidder, A. V.

1919 "Prehistoric Cultures of the San Juan Drainage." Nineteenth International Congress of Americanists, *Proceedings*, 108–13.

1927 "Southwestern Archaeological Conference." *Science*, LXVI, No. 1716, 489.

1936 *The Pueblo of Pecos*, Vol. 2. New Haven.

Kidder, A. V., and Guernsey, S. J.

1919 "Archaeological Excavations in Northeastern Arizona." Bureau of American Ethnology, *Bulletins*, No. 65.

King, Dale S.

1949 "Nalakihu." Museum of Northern Arizona, *Bulletin*, No. 23.

Lowie, R. H.

1929 *Are We Civilized?* New York.

Luzan, Diego

1929 *The Espejo Expedition into New Mexico*. The Quivira Society, Publication No. 1, 96.

Mc.Gregor, J. C.

1931 "Prehistoric Cotton Fabrics of Arizona." Museum of Northern Arizona, *Museum Notes*, IV, No. 2.

1936 "Dating the Eruption of Sunset Crater." *American Antiquity*, II, No. 1, 15–26.

1936 "The Culture of Sites Which Were Occupied Shortly Before the Eruption of Sunset Crater." Museum of Northern Arizona, *Bulletin*, No. 9.

1937 "Winona Village." Museum of Northern Arizona, *Bulletin*, No. 12.

1938 "How Some Important Pottery Types Were Dated." Museum of Northern Arizona, *Bulletin*, No. 13.

1943 "Burial of an Early American Magician." American Philosophical Society, *Proceedings*, LXXXVI, No. 2.

Mallory, Garrick

1886 "Pictographs of the North American Indians." Bureau of American Ethnology, *Fourth Annual Report*, 13.

Mearns, Edgar A.

1890 "Ancient Dwellings of the Rio Verde Valley." *Popular Science Monthly*, XXXVII, October, 54.

Mendeleff, Cosmos

1896 "Aboriginal Remains in Verde Valley, Arizona." Bureau of American Ethnology, *Thirteenth Annual Report*, 185.

Mendeleff, Victor

1891 "A Study of Pueblo Architecture." Bureau of American Ethnology, *Eighth Annual Report*, 13.

Morris, Earl

1928 "An Aboriginal Salt Mine at Camp Verde, Arizona." American Museum of Natural History, *Anthropological Papers*, XXX, Part II.

1936 "Archaeological Background of Dates in Early Arizona Chronology." *Tree Ring Bulletin*, II, No. 4.

Morss, Noel

1931 "Notes on the Archaeology of Kaibito and Rainbow Plateaus in Arizona." Harvard University, *Papers of the Peabody Museum of American Archaeology and Ethnology*, XII, No. 2.

Nelson, N. C.

1914 "Pueblo Ruins of the Galisteo Basin, New Mexico." American Museum of Natural History, *Anthropological Papers*, XV, Part I.

Nesbitt, Paul H.

1938 "Starkweather Ruin." Logan Museum, *Publications in Anthropology, Bulletin*, No. 6.

Pliny

1912 *The Letters of Caius Plinius Caecilius Secundus*, Tr. Melmoth, London.

Robinson, H. H.

1913 "The San Franciscan Mountain Volcanic Field, Arizona." U.S. Geological Survey, *Professional Papers*, No. 76.

Sauer, Carl

1935 *Ibero-Americano*, X, No. 8, 2.

INDEX